D1571376

Lent and Easter
in the Domestic Church

Lent and Easter
in the
Domestic Church

CATHERINE AND PETER FOURNIER

IGNATIUS PRESS   SAN FRANCISCO

"Mom, where's Heaven?"

"It's the light behind the night sky, that makes the stars . . ."

Family life is the journey toward heaven. To G. P., Granpa, Tante Faustina, Aunt Ena, who've gone ahead and are waiting for us.

Scripture quotations are from the Holy Bible, Revised Standard Version, Catholic Edition. Old Testament © 1952; Apocrypha © 1957; New Testament © 1946; Catholic Edition © 1965, by the Division of Christian Education of the National Council of the Churches of Christ in the United States of America. All rights reserved.

Exerpts from the English translation of the *Catechism of the Catholic Church* for use in the United States of America copyright © 1994, United States Catholic Conference, Inc.—Libreria Editrice Vaticana. English translation of the *Catechism of the Catholic Church: Modifications from the Editio Typica* copyright © 1997, United States Catholic Conference, Inc.—Libreria Editrice Vaticana. Used with permission.

"The Light of the World: Making a Paschal Candle" and "Have a Pentecost Feast" were written by Gwen Wise.

Illustrations by Catherine Fournier
Book design by Peter and Catherine Fournier

Copyright © 2002 by Domestic Church Communications Ltd., Peter W. A. Fournier and Catherine A. Fournier.
All rights reserved.

Published by Ignatius Press, San Francisco.

ISBN 0–89870–860–5
Library of Congress Control Number 2001088853

Printed in the United States of America ∞

Contents

LUKE 24:1-53. But on the first day of the week, at early dawn, they went to the tomb, taking the spices which they

Doing Better

One of my favorite Lenten traditions is not in this book. You see, we live in a small rural hamlet, about a twenty-minute drive from our parish church. I would like to go to daily Mass—I am sure it would do me immeasurable good—but it is not possible to coordinate Mass times with the school bus schedules, the part-time after-school work schedules, and all the rest of the activities of a busy family with two aging cars.

During Lent, though, we attend the Lenten Wednesday night Masses that our priest holds in the parish. Not only are these quiet evening Masses good altar-boy practice for my young sons, they are a calm, bright spot in the midst of our busy week. Our large church is almost empty at these Masses. There is no choir, no guitars, no jolly-friendly homily, just the Word and the Eucharist. And every Lenten Wednesday evening I realize that this is all that is necessary. Just the priest, my family, the Lord, and I. Everything else is extra. And sometimes a distracting extra.

Our small sacrifices of Lent—the organization to get us all out of the house on a Wednesday evening and myself to Friday afternoon Stations of the Cross, the time spent planning meatless meals, the abstinence from whatever habit needs bending, if not breaking (coffee, sweets, television), and our other Lenten practices—are all reminders of what is necessary and what is extra.

Lent is a penitential season. This does not mean it is a season for berating myself about what a sinner I am. Rather, it is a season for practicing doing better. Doing better at remembering the difference between necessary and extra. Doing better at following God's plan. Just doing better at being who we are. Jesus Christ and his bride, the Church, give us Lent as a special time to practice this in preparation for the great feast of Easter. (See CCC 1169.)

For me, getting to Mass twice a week, praying the Stations of the Cross on Friday afternoons, doing without coffee or chocolate, and relying on something other than caffeine or will power to get me through the day is doing better. Not best, but better. For you and your family, it will be something else.

Over the years, we have collected a number of activities to celebrate and observe Lent in the domestic church, things that help us all practice doing better. Some of them worked well when our children were little, while others were effective during those special Lenten seasons when we were preparing a child for First Confession and First Communion. (See CCC 2223, 2232.)

I have found that Lenten traditions can be a bit flexible—unlike Advent, for, once an Advent tradition has been added to your family observances, it is with you until all your children marry. Our family chooses three or four practices each year, things that suit the age range, interests, and abilities of the family at the time, and a different three or four the year after. One year we might abstain from desserts, pray the Stations of the Cross, and go to Wednesday night Mass. The next year, we might have more meatless meals, put the money saved in an alms box, do more volunteer work, and go to Wednesday night Mass.

This book shares some of the Lenten and Easter practices that have worked for our family and for others. We have included our favorite family activities, crafts for the whole family, and a number of pictures for the children to color. For additional copies of the coloring pictures and craft patterns, visit our "secret" web page at http://www.domestic-church.com/index.dir/index_ref_le.htm/. Some important feasts fall in Lent, and we have included them too, with information about traditional celebrations and some recipes for you to try. We have added many prayers, both for Lent and for the whole year. In addition, throughout the book, we have noted the numbers of relevant passages in the *Catechism of the Catholic Church* like this: (CCC 222).

I encourage you to try out the many activities in this book—but not all at once!—and develop your own Lenten practices, your own ways of doing better. See what happens in your own domestic church.

Peace,

Catherine

Family Activities

The Practice of Lenten Observances

The well-known and loved *Catechism of the Catholic Church* (and if you do not have one I urge you to buy one right away!) is an excellent resource for families. Rather than having a question-and-answer format, it is organized into four parts: The Profession of Faith, which examines the elements of our faith; The Celebration of the Christian Mystery, which describes and explains the sacraments; Life in Christ, which discusses man's vocation, the Ten Commandments, conscience, and morality; and Christian Prayer, which looks at the inestimable value of prayer. It has an answer for almost every "Mom, how come?" and "Dad, what does this mean?"

Still, even though the *Catechism* can answer our questions, families are often left wondering how to implement what they have learned. It is a fairly common challenge: How do we interpret a generalized teaching in specific circumstances? How do we bring the theoretical to practical life? How do we simplify a complex concept without losing the essential idea?

This challenge is especially pressing in family life. Family life can be described as the day-to-day activity of civilizing our small barbarians and passing our faith on to them. Families need to make the habits, customs, and practices of Catholic life interesting and memorable to their small children without making them bland, boring, and meaninglessly shallow to the bigger ones (including ourselves). Fortunately this is not difficult. Actively living our faith in daily life is enough to teach it to our children.

Of course this still leaves us with the "Yes, but how?" question unanswered. Especially how to observe the penitential season of Lent in the family. We are not secluded religious; we cannot expect our children to live on one meal of bread and water, nor can we suddenly impose a regime of prayer six times a day.

The following Lenten practice ideas answer the "How to" challenge by presenting, first, the overall objective of a fast and, then, by suggesting some ways to live a forty-day period of prayer, penance, and spiritual exercise. Since the season of Lent is in preparation for a proper celebration of the feast of Easter, daily life through Lent should reflect our desire to grow in understanding and gratitude for Christ's sacrifice. Actions and activities, both big and small, can help us do that.

There are several categories of Lenten observances: external and internal, fasts, acts, and prayers. It can get confusing.

What Is a Corporal or External Fast?

A corporal (or external) fast means abstaining from (avoiding) certain foods, drinks, or entertainment, such as music, television, or parties. This type of fast can be very effective in bringing an individual or family's attention toward Christ, especially if the abstinence is complemented with a positive activity. Substitute reading out loud for television or writing letters for parties. In our secular, materialistic world, this kind of fast is not well understood and is considered unusual or even unhealthy. Even abstaining from meat during Lent is considered a bit odd, and going any farther than that is considered fanatical. (Even though fasting is considered completely acceptable for other less spiritual reasons, like losing weight. Go figure. [Pun intended.])

How to Perform a Corporal or External Fast

- Take less of what you like (and, optionally, more of what you dislike) at meals.
- Abstain from meat or sweets.
- Take nothing to drink between meals except water.
- Do not use seasoning on your food today.
- Do not use any sweeteners with your food or drinks today.
- Avoid listening to the radio at all today.
- Take nothing to eat between meals today.
- Do not watch any TV or videos; instead, read the Passion of Christ in your Bible or missal, or read a classic book aloud to the family.
- Take only one helping of each item at meals today. Stop eating before you are full.
- Say an extra Rosary.

What Is a Spiritual or Internal Fast?

A spiritual (or internal) fast consists of abstinence from all evil, in other words, from sin. Saint John Chrysostom taught that the "value of fasting consists not so much in abstinence from food but rather in withdrawal from sinful practices". And Saint Basil the Great explains: "Turning away from all wickedness means keeping our tongue in check, restraining our anger, suppressing evil desires, and avoiding all gossip, lying, and swearing. To abstain from these things—herein lies the true value of [a] fast." (See also CCC 1430–33).

How to Perform a Spiritual or Internal Fast

- Do not do any unnecessary talking; instead, say little prayers throughout the day. (To aid in this, write them down and put them around the house and in your work place.)
- Remember to be patient today in all things.
- Do not make any complaints today.
- Restrain your anger, and go out of your way to be kind to the person who caused your anger.
- Do not be distracted with someone else's business.
- Avoid any gossip; instead say an extra Rosary to overcome this temptation.
- When asked to do something extra, do it with a joyful and pleasant attitude today. (Children can really understand this one.)
- Speak in a pleasant tone to everyone.
- Tell the truth in all your dealings.
- Do not look for praise today; instead, find an opportunity to praise someone else.

What Is Spiritual Change?

The development of virtues and habits of good works and prayer should be the main objective of any Lenten observance. The Fathers of the Church insisted that during Lent the faithful attend the Lenten church services and daily Mass.

Over the centuries since then Lenten observances, especially fasting, have undergone many changes. While it was once normal for most people to fast on bread and water during Lent, to reduce their hours of sleep, and to wear some form of penitential garment, today the observance of Lent is almost overlooked. Yet, the point of the exercise, the spiritual growth and change of life-style, is as important today as at any time in the history of the Church.

How to Develop Spiritual Change (Practice Virtues and Good Works)

- Practice humility in all your actions.
- Be generous today; help someone in need.
- Look for ways to be helpful throughout the day.
- Do a job that needs being done without being asked.
- Be courageous; walk away from any impure situations.
- Do not be at all idle or lazy. Always be doing something for others or for your own spiritual growth.
- Go out of your way today to help or talk to someone who is usually difficult.
- Volunteer for an extra job.
- Say an extra Rosary today for the conversion of a sinner.
- Visit someone who is sick or lonesome today. Offer to say the Rosary with the person.

When the general idea and purpose of a fast is presented and explained to children (of all ages) with clear and specific recommendations, they tend to embrace it enthusiastically.

If we can help them hold on to that enthusiasm for their faith practices through our support, encouragement, and example, we will learn and grow through Lent ourselves, as well.

The Family Altar

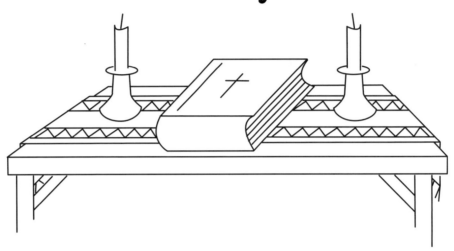

Lent has always been a time of increased reflection and prayer, a time for making new habits of prayer that we always hope will carry on into ordinary time. A family altar, or prayer table as some call it, helps not only to maintain a family habit of prayer, but serves as a physical reminder that our home is a place of worship. This is the whole idea of the domestic church, that we worship through our family life, in our homes. A family altar is the expression of that worship call.

This altar need not be anything elaborate, fancy, or expensive. If the home is full of small, inquisitive children with busy fingers, it need not even be a table-top altar. (For many years, our family altar was the top shelf of a bookcase, which in turn was bolted to the wall, because our hyperactive son was fond of climbing. I had nightmares about what would happen if he ever pulled it over on himself.) What is essential is that it be a place easily visible when the family gathers for prayers. A small table in a corner (where the TV used to sit?), or space on top of a bookcase or a mantel will work well.

Creating and maintaining a family altar is a simple activity but one that will make a difference to your family's prayer life and to the atmosphere of the home.

The family altar should include a few items to show that it is a special place:

- A cloth covering, either embroidered or in the liturgical color of the season, gives the family altar a certain formality and a freshness as the color changes with the season.
- A crucifix and small statues of favorite saints, along with votive lights or candlesticks, can then be arranged on the altar. During the Advent season, we put the Jesse Tree on the altar. The Advent wreath is also placed there when not on the table during meals.
- A Bible is an important addition. It can be opened to the reading of the day or to a favorite passage. Books of prayers or meditations can also be kept at the family altar for easy access at prayer time.
- Icons or pictures can be placed in stands or hung on the wall behind the family altar. Like the crucifix and statues, icons and pictures give focus to our meditations and devotions. The images used in icons always contain symbols that indicate some part of the Gospel story or the life of the saint.
- Last but not least the family altar is a good place to keep the family's rosaries ready for evening prayers. (It is better than having them spread all over the house.)

Fast, Abstinence, and Self-Denial in Lent—A Look at the Past

During this Lenten season, you might be interested in reading (and perhaps following?) the Lenten regulations from more than a hundred years ago.*

"The regulations for the keeping of Lent which begins next Wednesday are as follows:

"Persons obliged to fast must fast every day in Lent except Sundays. They can eat meat once a day except Wednesdays and Fridays, Ember Saturday and Holy Saturday. [Note: Ember Saturday is the first Saturday of Lent.]

"So—persons obliged to fast can eat meat as often as they like on Sundays, once on Mondays, Tuesdays, Thursdays and Saturdays except Saturday of Ember Week and Holy Saturday, but not at all on Wednesdays, Fridays, Ember Saturday or Holy Saturday.

"Persons fasting may take tea or coffee and a piece of bread in the morning, a full meal about noon, and eight ounces in the evening—eight ounces is a pretty fair allowance—but they should not drink milk in the morning except what they use in their tea, nor is it allowed to eat fish and meat at the same meal. They can use grease, lard and drippings in cooking fasting food.

"Persons under 21 and over 60 are not obliged to fast, neither are persons working so hard that they could not do their work fasting, nor women bearing or nursing their children. Persons not obliged to fast may eat meat as often as they like on the days that persons fasting are allowed to eat it once—but they are not allowed to eat meat on Wednesdays and Fridays.

"During Lent self-denial may be practised in many little acts but particularly in the avoidance of dangerous occasions of sin; such as, reading novels, attending dances, close company-keeping, glib-tongued-ness about one's neighbor and excessive use of liquor."

---

* From the February 22, 1885, bulletin of St. Patrick's Church, Mount St. Patrick, Ontario, Canada.

Almsgiving and Charity

Collecting money for the poor is another traditional Lenten activity, one that (for a variety of reasons) has not fallen into the same disfavor as fasting in modern times. What is not well understood is that in addition to the vital aspect of almsgiving—helping the poor—there is an equally important aspect that concerns helping ourselves. When we share, we all benefit in more than just feeling good. Almsgiving is an act of penance, a reparation for our sins and the sins of the world. Here is what the *Catechism of the Catholic Church* says about almsgiving and charity.

"*The seasons and days of penance* in the course of the liturgical year (Lent, and each Friday in memory of the death of the Lord) are intense moments of the Church's penitential practice [cf. SC 109–10; CIC, cann. 1249–53; CCEO, cann. 880–83]. These times are particularly appropriate for spiritual exercises, penitential liturgies, pilgrimages as signs of penance, voluntary self-denial such as fasting and almsgiving, and fraternal sharing (charitable and missionary works)" (CCC 1438).

"The theological virtues of faith, hope, and charity inform and give life to the moral virtues. Thus charity leads us to render to God what we as creatures owe him in all justice. The *virtue of religion* disposes us to have this attitude" (CCC 2095).

"The corporal works of mercy consist especially in feeding the hungry, sheltering the homeless, clothing the naked, visiting the sick and imprisoned, and burying the dead [cf. Mt 25:31–46]. Among all these, giving alms to the poor is one of the chief witnesses to fraternal charity: it is also a work of justice pleasing to God [cf. Tob 4:5–11; Sir 17:22; Mt 6:2–4]:

'He who has two coats, let him share with him who has none; and he who has food must do likewise' [Lk 3:11]. 'But give for alms those things which are within; and behold, everything is clean for you' [Lk 11:41]. 'If a brother or sister is ill-clad and in lack of daily food, and one of you says to them, "Go in peace, be warmed and filled," without giving them the things needed for the body, what does it profit?' [Jas 2:15–16; cf. 1 Jn 3:17]". (CCC 2447.)

in deed and word before God and all the people, and how our chief priests and rulers delivered him up to be condemned to death, and crucified him. But we had hoped that he was

Shrove Tuesday

I remember Pancake Day from my childhood. It seemed a bizarre tradition, one that turned my mother's nutritional schedule upside down and one that transformed math class into a picnic. Though I asked, there was little or no explanation for the inexplicable adult actions. Of course, offered plates of pancakes brimming with butter and dripping with syrup, I did not question the matter too closely.

During my first Lenten season as a Catholic, I finally began to gain some understanding and explanation for this strange habit. Actually it is not so strange at all; it makes perfect sense when viewed in a liturgical light, as does all of Catholic tradition.

Shrove Tuesday (also known as Fat Tuesday, Mardi Gras, or *fetter Dienstag*) is the day before Ash Wednesday, the beginning of Lent. Since Lent is a time of abstinence, traditionally from meat, fat, eggs, and dairy products (one wonders what was left), Shrove Tuesday's menu was designed to use up all the fat, eggs, and dairy products left in the kitchen and storeroom. It is also a "feast" to prepare for the time of "famine" in the desert. In some cultures, it is traditional to eat as much as possible on Shrove Tuesday, sometimes up to twelve times over the course of the whole day.

The English terms "shrovetide" and "Shrove Tuesday" are from the word *shrive*, which is described in the Webster's dictionary as an archaic term that means both to hear and make a confession and to give and receive absolution. Since confession is a preparation for the receiving of Communion, Shrove Tuesday is a preparation for the beginning of Lent and the great feast of Easter.

In many traditions, Lent is a time for cleaning in preparation for Easter and spring. First one's soul, then the kitchen, then the rest of the house was cleansed and purified of the past year's accumulations. Old clothes were mended and new clothes purchased at this time of year. In the Ukraine, houses were whitewashed inside and out during Lent. In this way, everything was made ready to face the season of Salvation

and Rebirth. Traditions of spring cleaning stem from this Lenten religious observance.

The recipes given will make about ten pancakes—enough for three people. Throw cholesterol concern to the winds, and have lots of bacon too!

Plain Mlyntsi (Griddle Cakes)

Ingredients
- 1 cup flour
- ½ teaspoon salt
- 2 teaspoons baking powder
- ½ teaspoon sugar
- 1 tablespoon melted butter
- 1 egg
- ¾ cup milk

Directions

Place the dry ingredients in a bowl, and stir them together well with a fork.

Add the remaining ingredients, and beat well with a manual or electric beater until thoroughly blended.

Heat a heavy griddle or frying pan (cast iron is best). Grease the pan lightly with a few drops of oil.

Test the griddle with a few drops of cold water. The griddle is hot enough when the drops keep a globular shape and skitter across the pan. If the water spreads out, the pan is too cool. If the drops evaporate immediately, the pan is too hot and the cakes will burn.

Pour the batter into the pan with a small scoop or measuring cup to form cakes about 3 inches in diameter.

Cook the cakes until bubbles break on the surface, flip them quickly, and cook the other side. Do not turn more than once.

Serve very hot with syrup, honey, or corn syrup and thick sour cream or yogurt.

Oatmeal Apple Pancakes

Ingredients

- 1 cup oatmeal
- 2 cups buttermilk or sour milk (1 cup milk plus 1 tablespoon lemon juice)
- 2 eggs
- 2 tablespoons oil
- 1 teaspoon cinnamon, if desired
- 1 cup flour
- 2 teaspoons salt
- 2 teaspoons baking soda
- 1 apple, cored, peeled, and chopped into small pieces

Directions

Place the oatmeal and buttermilk together in a large bowl.

Allow to soak for a few minutes.

Add the eggs and oil and cinnamon (if using). Stir well.

Add the flour, salt, baking soda, and apple. Stir until blended.

Heat a heavy frying pan. Grease lightly with oil.

Pour about ⅓ cup batter into the pan with a small measuring cup.

Bake the pancake until bubbles break on the surface, flip quickly, and bake the other side. Make sure the pancakes are baked through.

Keep the pancakes warm in a warm oven until all are done.

Serve hot.

Hot Honey Butter Sauce

Ingredients

- ½ cup cold water
- 1 tablespoon cornstarch
- ½ cup honey
- 2 tablespoons butter
- 1 teaspoon lemon juice

Directions

In a small saucepan, mix together the cold water and cornstarch.

Stir in the honey and butter, and cook over low heat until butter is melted and sauce is thickened.

Add the lemon juice. Serve hot on pancakes or apple dumplings, butter cake or anything else that appeals to you.

Potato Pancakes

Crisp and brown, these are great with sour cream or yogurt, bacon, and applesauce. This year, I am going to try cooking them in the waffle iron.

Ingredients

- 3 medium potatoes
- 1 tablespoon flour
- 1 tablespoon cream
- 1 egg, beaten
- Salt
- 4 tablespoons bacon fat or oil

Directions

Wash and grate the potatoes. Place the potatoes on a double thickness of paper towels, fold the towels around them, and twist and squeeze until most of the moisture is removed.

Unwrap the potatoes and dump them in a bowl. Add the flour, cream, egg, and salt, and toss until mixed.

Heat the fat or oil in a skillet.

Put about 2 tablespoons of the potato mixture in the pan. Press and shape the pancakes into a flat 3½-inch cake.

Repeat until pan is full but not crowded. Cook each pancake about 5 minutes over medium-low heat until the bottom is crisp and brown. Turn and cook the other side for 5 minutes more.

Keep warm in a 300°F oven until all are ready. Serve.

him they did not see." And he said to them, "O foolish men, and slow of heart to believe all that the prophets have spoken! Was it not necessary that the Christ should suffer

The Lenten Cross

This family activity is similar to the Jesse Tree used at Advent. The Jesse Tree follows both the family tree of Jesus and the history of the first Advent, when God's people awaited the coming of the Messiah. The Lenten Cross simultaneously follows the messianic prophecies through the Old Testament and its fulfillment in the Crucifixion narrative. It is a way to bring the Gospel narrative to life for children and to teach the whole family that God's plan for His people extends through all of history.

For obvious reasons, the Lenten Cross is in the shape of a cross. Proportions of four units by two units for the each cross piece and twelve units by two units for the upright gives a well-proportioned cross. Divide the cross into forty sections as shown in the illustration, leaving a large center section for an image of the resurrected Christ on Easter morning.

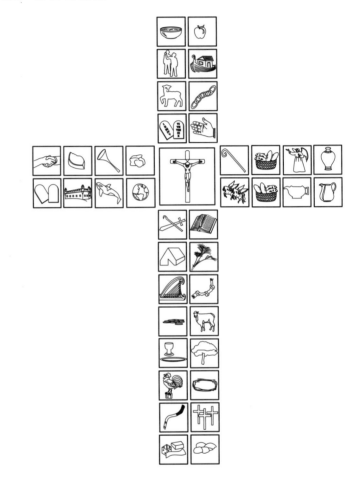

Your family Lenten Cross can be made of almost anything. Some options are: a banner with Velcro dots for fastening, a wooden cross with small nails or hooks, or a laminated cardboard poster with reusable sticky putty. Whatever your budget and ability can create will be welcomed as a new family tradition. Do not worry if you are not an artist; children are wonderfully tolerant of Mom and Dad's "production quality"! The images representing each daily reading can be painted on disks of wood, embroidered on small pieces of canvas, or drawn onto cardboard. For this article, I will call these small images icons.

There a few ways to add the icons to the Lenten Cross. An icon can be added to the cross every day as the reading is done, as with the Jesse Tree, or each icon can be flipped over from a blank side to the picture side after the prayer is read. A visually exciting idea is to have the individual images on one side of each icon and a large image, of Christ for example, made from the forty pieces, on the back of each piece. As the icons are flipped, a picture of Christ slowly emerges.

The Lenten Cross begins on Ash Wednesday, skips the Sundays of Lent (because they are not part of Lent—an idea that completely confused me the first Lent after my conversion), and ends on Holy Saturday.

The Lenten Cross adds regular Scripture reading and prayer to your Lenten observances, giving the interest and continuity of a developing story through the season. It really is the greatest story ever told.

Lenten Cross Readings
Days 1 to 4

Ash Wednesday
Even Now (Joel 2:12–13)

3rd Day of Lent
Cain and Abel (Genesis 4:1–12)

2d Day of Lent
Original Sin (Genesis 3:1–20)

4th Day of Lent
Noah's Ark (Genesis 6:5–13, 9:8–11)

Lenten Cross Readings
Days 5 to 10

5th Day of Lent
Abraham and Isaac (Genesis 22:1–18)

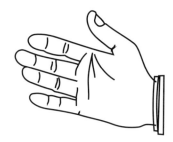

8th Day of Lent
The Covenant with Abraham and Moses
(Jeremiah 31:31–33)

6th Day of Lent
Jesus and Abraham (John 8:31–40)

9th Day of Lent
A New Covenant (Luke 22:15–20)

7th Day of Lent
Moses and the Ten Commandments
(Exodus 20:1–21)

10th Day of Lent
Two Great Commandments
(Matthew 22:34–40)

Lent and Easter in the Domestic Church: Family Activities www.Domestic-Church.com

Lenten Cross Readings
Days 11 to 16

11th Day of Lent
Forty Years in the Desert
(Numbers 14:2–4, 10–12, 17–19, 33–34)

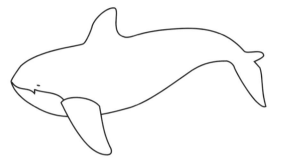

14th Day of Lent
Jonah and the Whale (Jonah 1:1—4:11)

12th Day of Lent
Forty Days in the Desert (Luke 4:1–13)

15th Day of Lent
Whom Shall I Send? (Isaiah 6:8–10)

13th Day of Lent
Moses and the Ten Commandments
(Exodus 20:1–21)

16th Day of Lent
Trust and Rescue (Psalm 22)

Lenten Cross Readings
Days 17 to 22

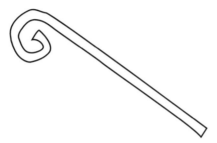

17th Day of Lent
Prophetic Rule of Jeremiah
(Jeremiah 1:4–8, 3:12–15)

18th Day of Lent
Story of Elijah (2 Kings 2:9–12)

19th Day of Lent
Story of Elisha (2 Kings 4:38–44)

20th Day of Lent
Loaves and Fishes (Mark 6:34–44)

21st Day of Lent
Gabriel and the Anointed One
(Daniel 9:15–24)

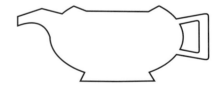

22nd Day of Lent
Anointing of David (1 Samuel 16:1–13)

Lent and Easter in the Domestic Church: Family Activities

Lenten Cross Readings
Days 23 to 28

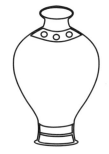

23rd Day of Lent
Anointing at Bethany
(Matthew 26:6–13)

26th Day of Lent
Filfillment of All Prophecies
(Luke 24:44–48)

24th Day of Lent
John the Baptist
(Luke 1:13–17, 80)

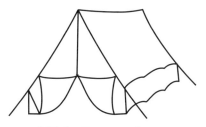

27th Day of Lent
Transfiguration (Luke 9:28–36)

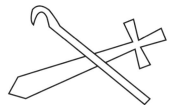

25th Day of Lent
Prophecy of New Order (Micah 4:1–7)

28th Day of Lent
Entrance into Jerusalem (Matthew 21:1–9)

Lenten Cross Readings
Days 29 to 34

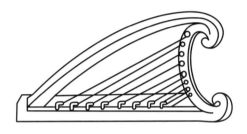

29th Day of Lent
Zeal for Your House (Psalm 69:6–25)

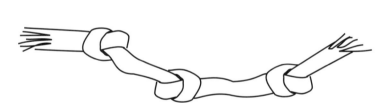

30th Day of Lent
The Money Lenders in the Temple
(John 2:13–25)

31st Day of Lent
Judas (Matthew 26:14–25)

32nd Day of Lent
The Innocent Victim (Isaiah 53:1–12)

33th Day of Lent
The Last Supper (Luke 22:14–20)

34th Day of Lent
The Agony in the Garden (Matthew 26:36–46)

Lenten Cross Readings
Days 35 to 40

35th Day of Lent
Denial of Jesus
(Mark 14:29–31, 66–72)

38th Day of Lent
The Two Thieves
(Luke 23:32–43)

36th Day of Lent
The Crown of Thorns
(Matthew 27:27–31)

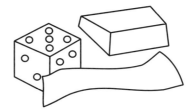

39th Day of Lent
On the Cross
(John 19:23–27)

37th Day of Lent
Scourging at the Pillar (John 19:1–7)

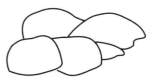

40th Day of Lent
Death of Jesus (Matthew 27:45–54)

the scriptures the things concerning himself. So they drew near to the village to which they were going. He appeared to be going further, but they constrained him, saying, "Stay

Fasting with Homemade Bread

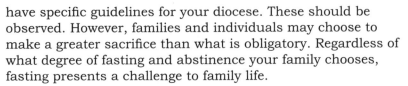

The *Code of Canon Law* (another excellent resource for families) sets out the regulations of the Church. Among the laws are those concerning penance, fasting, and abstinence.

Why should we do penance? Divine law obliges all Christ's faithful to do penance. While everyone can perform penance in his own way, there are certain specified days of penance, so that the Church community is joined together in a communal practice of penance. On these days, the community should spend time in prayer, participate in projects of piety and charity, and abstain and fast when required.

When should we do penance? The Code identifies these common days of penance as each Friday of the whole year and the whole of the season of Lent.

What is meant by fasting and abstaining? In the universal Church, abstinence from eating meat is observed on Fridays throughout the year, not only those of Lent. Fasting means reducing the amount of food and number of meals eaten in the day. Both abstinence and fasting are to be observed on Ash Wednesday and Good Friday.

Who should fast? Canon Law states that at least all those past their fourteenth birthday should abstain, although younger children may also abstain. Fasting is expected of adults until age sixty. Persons older and younger than this may also choose to fast, although it is not required. Priests and parents should make sure those in their care not required to fast and abstain understand the intent and meaning of penance.

We are asked to fast and abstain during Lent as penance and sacrifice (CCC 1434, 2043). Fasting generally means eating simpler and smaller meals, and abstaining generally refers to removing meat from the meal. Some individuals or families may choose to fast on the weekdays throughout Lent, not just on Ash Wednesday and Good Friday. Some may choose to have only one meal a day while fasting—to share the life of the poor, who have little to eat. Others may choose to abstain from meat throughout Lent or some other variation. Your bishop may have specific guidelines for your diocese. These should be observed. However, families and individuals may choose to make a greater sacrifice than what is obligatory. Regardless of what degree of fasting and abstinence your family chooses, fasting presents a challenge to family life.

Some members of the family—children, pregnant or nursing women, and aged relatives—cannot and should not fast. So, a meal needs to be prepared for them. Family members who are fasting need nutritious and satisfying food for their simple meals. Homemade bread and homemade soup satisfy these requirements. And if it is going to be bread, it really should be good bread. Homemade bread is so much better than store-bought bread that after a while the soft, pallid, tasteless stuff from the store is not recognizable as deserving the label bread. And it is truly easy to make, regardless of your schedule, budget, or physical limitations.

A bread-maker is unnecessary. Loaf pans are unnecessary. An oven is unnecessary for some kinds of bread. Even yeast is optional. The absolute minimum for bread making is flour, water, and a heat source. Pita, bannock, and chapatis are simple kinds of bread made on a hot surface without yeast. Sourdough bread is made with a "wild" yeast culture (yeast captured from the air and grown on a medium or food source). Quick breads use baking powder or baking soda as leavening.

Anyone can make bread, and everyone can help make bread. Adding flour, mixing, kneading, watching, and finally shaping into loaves and baking: bread making can be a true family activity.

Making Bread

The following recipe will seem long, but in actual practice it is extremely simple. It uses a bare-bones list of ingredients, producing the very simplest, plainest bread possible. It will still taste wonderful and homemade. A slightly more elaborate recipe follows these directions.

I am giving the instructions in some detail so that every step is clear. Once this recipe is mastered, you will be able to bake virtually any bread recipe with confidence. The ingredients given will make two loaves.

Simple White Bread

Ingredients
- 2 cups warm (100°F; 37°C) water
- 1 tablespoon dry yeast
- 4 to 6 cups flour (White flour will work best, though whole wheat is healthier. If you want to use whole wheat flour, try a 3:1 white to whole wheat mix to begin with.)
- 2 teaspoons salt

Directions

Pour the warm water into a large mixing bowl. The temperature of the water is important. Yeast is a living plant. A temperature that is too warm will kill it (that is what happens when you finally put it in the oven), and one that is too cold will keep it from growing quickly. It is better to err on the side of too cold rather than too hot. As the yeast grows, it gives off carbon dioxide, which forms bubbles in the batter—this is the rising that gives bread its lightness. Once you understand this, everything else in bread making makes sense.

Sprinkle the dry yeast over the water. Dry yeast is in suspended animation and will keep for some time if kept dry. Once it

touches water, it wakes up and starts growing. Sprinkling it over the water gets it started and well dissolved into the water. Leave it alone for a few minutes until the water, when stirred, looks cloudy in a light beige shade. If you add a little sugar (a food source for the yeast) to this water, it will dissolve more quickly and will bubble and froth. Exciting.

When the yeast is dissolved, add two cups of flour and the salt. Beat very well. This step begins the batter. Vigorous beating (you cannot beat it too long) at this stage develops the gluten in the flour and gives the bread a nice springy texture. Gluten is a protein, a long, twisted, stringlike molecule. It dissolves out of the flour when mixed with water. Energetic beating dissolves more of the gluten into the batter and helps all the strings arrange themselves. They form a honeycombed texture that holds the bubbles of gas given off by the yeast. A high-powered electric beater does the job nicely. You have beaten enough when the dough is stretchy and falls in long thick ropes from your spoon when you lift it out of the bowl. The surface will be slightly rough and shiny. This step may take three to five minutes.

Add the rest of the flour, a little at a time, beating it in well. When the dough is too stiff to stir any more and pulls away from the sides of the bowl, sprinkle a bit of flour on the counter and dump it out. **Caution:** You will have to stop using your electric mixer at some point unless you have a bread-hook attachment. Otherwise, when the batter becomes stiff, you will burn out the motor.

Now you start kneading. Kneading accomplishes two purposes. It works the last of the flour into the dough, and it develops the gluten even more. As you knead the bread it will gradually transform from a lumpy sticky mass into a silky smooth tight ball. The more flour you add, the harder and more crumbly your bread will be. The less flour, the softer (and less easy to slice thinly) the bread will be. You need a balance between the two undesirable extremes, but fortunately the in-between area is very large.

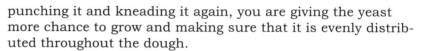

scriptures?" And they rose that same hour and returned to Jerusalem; and they found the eleven gathered together and those who were with them, who said, "The Lord has risen

To knead bread, the basic movement is pushing down and away, then folding back and toward you. Give it a quarter turn each time. It can develop into a rocking movement, down and away, back and toward. Unless you are tall (about 5′8″ and above) a typical kitchen counter is too high to be comfortable. Try your kitchen table. Lightly flour your surface and begin kneading. If the bread dough sticks, sprinkle a little more flour on it. As the bread develops, it will become less sticky, so be careful not to add too much flour at the beginning; the bread may not need it. Rub your hands together (as if you were washing them) over the dough occasionally if the bits stuck to your palms bother you.

When the dough is kneaded enough, the surface will form blisters, bubbles that develop under the surface and break as the dough is stretched. It will feel smooth and bouncy and will be about the firmness of a baby's bottom. Really. If it is harder than that, more like a toddler's muscled bottom, you have added too much flour. If it feels like your belly immediately after giving birth, you have not added enough flour.

When you think you have kneaded it enough, put it back into the mixing bowl, which should still have some flour coating the sides, or into a clean, lightly greased bowl. Cover with a damp tea towel and put it to rise. If you put it in the refrigerator, it will rise very slowly and be risen enough in about eight hours (i.e., overnight). If you leave it on your counter on a cool day, it will rise gently and be risen enough in about two to four hours (i.e., long enough to go shopping or have a nap). If you put it in a warm place, in a gas oven with the pilot light on, on top of an electric oven turned on to 100°F (37°C), or in a warming closet (British moms will know what that is), it will rise in about an hour (i.e., long enough to clean up the kitchen and start some laundry).

When the dough has risen to twice its size, give it a good punch. It will sigh gently and collapse on itself. This is the yeast bubbles collapsing. You are doing this because, while it has risen, there are not enough little yeast plants in it yet, and each bubble is too big to make nicely textured bread. You want more yeast plants and smaller bubbles. By

punching it and kneading it again, you are giving the yeast more chance to grow and making sure that it is evenly distributed throughout the dough.

Knead the bread dough a few times, just enough to get it smooth and even. Cut it into two even pieces, and cover them again with the damp tea towel while you grease the loaf pans. If you do not have loaf pans, grease some cookie sheets or two frying pans or two large (48 fl. oz.) apple or tomato juice cans. Juice cans are especially good for large batches—eight juice cans will fit into an oven that will only take three or four loaf pans. Grease cans very well with white vegetable shortening.

Knead and shape each loaf into a smooth slightly cylindrical shape by patting it into a rough rectangle and folding it together. Pinch the long edge together and smooth the top side. If you are using a cookie sheet or frying pan, make round loaves.

Place the loaves into the pans. People from many Catholic countries make a sign of the cross over bread when it is set to rise. A Portuguese prayer says, "May this bread rise in the pan as the wheat rises in the field, O Lord. Amen."

Set the loaves to rise again until doubled. They will rise more quickly this time, so check them after about an hour. (More laundry and start dinner.) You do not want them to rise too much, because they will also rise in the oven at first, and if they go in too big, they will rise too far, overflow the pans, and generally look horrible. If your loaves over-rise, punch them down and start again.

Preheat the oven to 350°F. Bake the bread for 25 to 30 minutes. The baking time will depend on the size of the loaves, the consistency of the dough, and the age of your oven. Check them after 25 minutes. The loaves should have nicely browned tops and have shrunk slightly away from the sides of the pan. Take one loaf out of the oven and slide it out of the pan. Tap its bottom. If it produces a hollow "thunk" sound, the loaves are done. It will take some practice to distinguish the dull thud of an undone loaf from the hollow thump of a done one.

Remove the bread from the oven, slide the loaves out of the pans, and cool them on a wire rack. This is important; escaping steam can make the crust soggy and damp. If the crust seems too hard, you can brush the loaves with melted butter to soften it or cover the cooling loaves with a tea towel. When the bread is completely cool, put the loaves in paper or plastic bags and store in a bread box or in the refrigerator.

Basic White Bread

Ingredients

- 2 cups warm (100°F; 37°C) water plus ½ cup dry milk, or 2 cups warm milk (milk gives the bread a softer crumb and extra nutrition)
- 1 tablespoon dried yeast
- 2 tablespoons honey, brown or white sugar, corn syrup, or molasses (this makes the bread a bit sweeter)
- 2 tablespoons light oil, melted butter, or melted shortening (this gives the bread a softer crust)
- 2 tablespoons salt
- 5 to 6 cups flour
- 2 tablespoons wheat germ (optional)

Directions

Follow the directions given in the long text above, with these modifications:
- Add the sweetener and dry milk to the water before the yeast, or, if using milk, add the sweetener before adding the yeast.
- Add the oil with the salt and first amount of flour.

Some Favorite Additions

For a two-loaf recipe use:
- ½ cup mashed potatoes, melted butter (instead of oil), and 2 eggs, or,
- 1 cup cornmeal, melted shortening (instead of oil), and white sugar, or,
- 4 cups grated cheese and milk (instead of water), or
- 2 cups whole wheat flour, 4 cups white flour, honey (instead of sugar), and 2 cups raisins.

Grace at Meals

If the father of the family is absent, have the oldest male present say Grace. This serves as excellent training for the sons, who will some-day be priests—of a parish or a domestic church.

Bless us, O Lord, and these Thy gifts,
Which we are about to receive
From Thy bounty, through Christ, our Lord. Amen.

In Latin:
Benedic, Domine, nos et haec
Tua dona quae de
Tua largitate sumus sumpturi.
Per Christum Dominum nostrum. Amen.

Before we eat this food, dear Lord,
We bow our heads to pray;
And for Your blessings and Your care
Our humble thanks we say. Amen.

Come Lord Jesus, be our guest,
And let this food to us be blessed. Amen.

Thank You for the food we eat,
Thank You for the friends we meet.
Thank You for the birds that sing,
Thank You, God, for everything. Amen.

Gracious Giver of all good,
We thank You for rest and food;
Grant that all we do or say
May serve You joyfully today. Amen.

Thank You for the food we eat.
Thank You for the friends we meet.
Thank You for the sun above.
Thank You, God, for your love. Amen.

himself stood among them and said to them, "Peace to you." But they were startled and frightened, and supposed that

hands and my feet, that it is I myself; handle me, and see; for a spirit has not flesh and bones as you see that I have." And when he had said this he showed them his hands and

Going to Confession

When my husband and I visited Rome in October of the Millennium Jubilee Year, we decided to let the Holy Spirit be our tour guide. Rather than get drawn into the stress of keeping to an itinerary, we just wandered and saw what God wanted to show us.

We made only a few requests of our "tour guide". We wanted to go to confession at Saint Peter's and to attend a Mass there too. On our first visit (we spent a total of three days there), we found that an entire arm of the huge cross of Saint Peter's floorplan was dedicated to confessions—with confessionals lining the walls, all marked with the languages of the priest attending, and rows of pews in the middle.

I knelt in front of a huge painting of the Crucifixion and prepared myself with an examination of conscience. I grew steadily more and more nervous. When a woman left and walked away from a confessional marked English, I jumped to my feet and hurried over. I knew if I waited any longer, I would be too nervous to make a good confession.

For all that, when I was finally kneeling inside the confessional, my mind went completely blank. I managed to stammer out, "I am sorry, Father, I am so nervous, I do not know what to say." A rich Irish accent answered me, "Oh, stop. You will make me nervous next." I laughed, relaxed immediately, and made my confession.

If you were to ask someone to name a Lenten practice off the top of his head, about half would answer, "Going without candy/chocolate/coffee." The other half would probably suggest, "Going to confession."

The season of Lent is a time of penitential preparation for the sorrow of Good Friday and the joy of Easter Sunday. It is a natural time to begin or continue a habit of regular confession because this is a natural extension of the practice of external and internal fasts and of spiritual change (CCC 1440–49). Fasts and change require self-awareness, self-examination, and a sincere desire to reform. They also encourage awareness and sorrow for the moments when we do not follow Christ's example.

First admitting and then confessing our sins can be a painful yet liberating experience. Forgiveness and absolution give us the strength and courage to try again. A careful examination of conscience is essential for a good, complete confession (see CCC 1454).

An Examination of Conscience

An examination of conscience is a series of questions, intended to trigger our memory or lead our thoughts to a deeper understanding of our actions, in order to hand them over to God. Most examinations of conscience use the Ten Commandments as a starting point or organizational structure for the series of questions, since they are the clearest expression of God's wishes for our life.

The Ten Commandments of God

1. I am the Lord your God; you shall not have strange gods before Me.
2. You shall not take the name of the Lord your God in vain.
3. Remember to keep holy the Lord's day.
4. Honor your father and your mother.
5. You shall not kill.
6. You shall not commit adultery.
7. You shall not steal.
8. You shall not bear false witness against your neighbor.
9. You shall not covet your neighbor's wife.
10. You shall not covet your neighbor's goods.

In everyday life and especially with respect to the sacrament of confession, it is important that we form a clear and correct conscience. A properly formed conscience will help us in discerning whether we have obeyed God's commandments and how we can improve in submission to God's will. We must cultivate a judgment of ourselves that is both aware of offenses against the divine will and, at the same time, alert to the lies of the evil one.

A priest friend of our family recommended a highly effective way to distinguish thoughts, actions, and attitudes that are the result of a properly ordered conscience. It is characteristic of God and His angels to give true happiness and spiritual joy. It is similarly characteristic of the evil one to disrupt or destroy such happiness and consolation by proposing false reasonings, subtleties, and continual deceptions.

What can we conclude from this? That the more we try to please God in our lives, the more He will give us a deep interior peacefulness. We should suspect a temptation from the evil one when we find ourselves chronically worried or anxious or disturbed, no matter how pious or righteous the source of the worry or anxiety may appear to be. So one basic virtue on which we should daily examine ourselves is peace of soul. We should ask ourselves, "Have I given in to worry or anxiety?" "Have I allowed myself to get discouraged?" A good practice is to pronounce the name "Jesus" when we find ourselves getting despondent or to say a short aspiration, such as "My Jesus, I trust in You", whenever we become dejected over something.

There are many examinations of conscience. Some are written specifically for women or men, for workers or religious, or for young or old. Others take a more general approach, seeking to be of service to all. Here are two such examinations of conscience, first for adults and then for children. May we all grow closer to Christ and meet each other at His Throne!

Prayer before Confession

O God, give me the vision to see myself as You see me.

O Jesus, give me the grace to be truly sorry for my sins.

O Holy Spirit, give me the ability to express my contrition.

O Mary, help me to make a good confession.

Amen.

Examination of Conscience for Adults
Based on the Commandments

In order to make a good confession, besides confessing the nature or types of our sins, we should also try to remember the times we have committed these sins. There may also be circumstances that increase the severity of these sins, perhaps making a venial sin mortal or making a mortal sin worse. To prepare for our confession and remember the nature and number of our sins, we can ask ourselves a series of questions.*

1. Have I ever avoided confessing a sin or, while confessing, minimized it?
2. Have I ever neglected a careful examination of conscience before confession?
3. Have I ever skipped or skimped on my penance?
4. Have I failed in the obligation to make a confession and receive Holy Communion at least once a year?
5. Are any of my sins habitual? Have I ever confessed these habits?

First Commandment

1. Have I been generous and willing in my duties and obligations toward God? Do I remember to say my usual prayers?
2. Have I ever received Holy Communion while in a state of sin? Have I ever missed the one-hour fast before receiving Communion?
3. Do I deny God through belief in or activities of superstition and the occult?
4. Do I ever seriously doubt matters of faith? Do I protect my faith by avoiding material that contains errors or subjects contrary to Catholic faith and morals? Do I protect my faith by avoiding organizations contrary to Catholic faith and morals?
5. Have I committed sacrilege, that is, behaved in a disrespectful way toward a sacred person, place, or thing?

---

* Adapted from *Guidebook for Confession: The How and Why of the Sacrament of Reconciliation*, by Father Luis Esteban Latore, M.A., S.T.D., 3d English ed. (Greenhills, Philippines: Sinag-Tala Publishers, 1982).

Second Commandment

1. Do I try my best to keep the promises I have made to God?
2. Have I taken the name of the Lord in vain, that is, used God's name in an irreverent way by swearing, joking, or exclaiming? Have I used the names of the Blessed Virgin Mary or the saints in this way?
3. Have I been a sponsor in ceremonies of organizations with teachings contrary to the Catholic faith?
4. Have I always told the truth? Have I told the truth under oath?
5. Have I kept all my promises or vows I have made to others, either publicly or privately?

Third Commandment

1. Have I missed Mass on Sundays or holy days of obligation, either deliberately or by not planning well enough? Have I been late for Mass without good reason? Have I been so late that I missed my Sunday obligation?
2. Have I been distracted during Mass, either deliberately or by letting my mind wander away from the altar? Have I distracted others during Mass, either deliberately or by being distracted myself?
3. Do I help the Church as generously as I can?
4. Do I fast and abstain on the days the Church asks?
5. Do I avoid unnecessary work on Sundays and not make others work on Sunday?

Fourth Commandment

1. Have I taught my children how to live as Christians? Have I taught them their prayers? Have I taken them to church?
2. Have I made sure my children receive instruction in the sacraments and receive Baptism, First Confession, First Holy Communion, and Confirmation at appropriate times?
3. Do I give my children a good example of how to live as a Christian with my words and actions?
4. Do I protect my children's faith by monitoring the books they read, movies they watch, music they listen to, and the friends they keep?

Fifth Commandment

1. Have I injured others with my words: by losing my temper, being angry, envious or jealous, by teasing or insulting others, or by causing scandal with my speech?
2. Have I injured others with my actions: by reckless driving, fighting, having or recommending an abortion, or encouraging others to take drugs or to drink to excess?
3. Have I injured myself by taking drugs, drinking to excess, eating to excess, mutilating myself, fighting, or having an abortion?
4. Have I injured myself or others through having or recommending sterilization?
5. When I cause injury to others, either deliberately or accidentally, do I ask pardon?

Sixth and Ninth Commandments

1. Have I tried to keep my thoughts and mind pure by avoiding indecent thoughts and immoral books, movies, or pictures and by keeping the example of the Blessed Virgin and the saints before me at all times?
2. Have I tried to keep my words and speech pure by avoiding impure conversations and not leading others into impure conversations?
3. Have I always acted in a modest and pure manner, remembering that God is always near?
4. Have I guarded my modesty and the modesty of others by avoiding near occasions of sin, dressing modestly, and not encouraging others to behave immodestly?
5. Do I maintain a generous attitude toward new life by using Natural Family Planning in a responsible way and by not using artificial contraception or recommending it to others?

Seventh and Tenth Commandments

1. Am I honest or have I taken, either deliberately or accidentally, something that doesn't belong to me? Have I stolen anything by deception, fraud, or coercion?
2. Am I a good steward of my money or do I spend beyond my means? Do I pay my debts on time and in full?

3. Am I conscientious in my work and studies or am I lazy and neglectful?
4. Do I remember to respect other's property or have I damaged something belonging to someone else?
5. Am I glad for the successes of others, or do I envy them their success and possessions?

Eighth Commandment

1. Do I speak honestly at all times or do I tell lies? Do I tell harmful lies about others? Have I ever unjustly accused someone?
2. Do I respect other's privacy and not reveal their secrets?
3. Do I indulge in gossip and tale-telling? Do I tell the faults of others without reason?
4. Do I expect the best of everyone or have I judged others unfairly or held a grudge against someone?
5. If I have lied, gossiped, or told secrets, have I apologized and made whatever repairs I could?

> ### Prayer for a Good Confession
>
> Have mercy on me, O God, according to thy steadfast love; according to thine abundant mercy blot out my transgressions. Wash me thoroughly from my iniquity, and cleanse me from my sin! (Psalm 51:1–2)

Children's Examination of Conscience

Children should also be taught that an important part of preparation for confession is an examination of conscience, whether it is their first or their fortieth. This is not something they must memorize; their examination of conscience is to help them remember all the things they want to tell Jesus. It is even more important than the weekly phone call to Grandma or the letter to Saint Nicholas during Advent!

It is easy, though, to be distracted or forgetful while doing an examination of conscience. For this reason, lists of recommended questions or meditations are created. The basic outline usually follows the Ten Commandments. These also provide a good framework for teaching your child about confession and teaching an early or simple definition of sin. The following is an examination of conscience created for children. Even this examination of conscience can be bit dry for younger children. As a parent you will probably want to add some specifics. For example, "Did I feed the fish/dog/cat/ferret/gerbil/bird/cricket every day?" if your child has a pet.

Responsibilities to God

1. Have I prayed every day?
2. Have I prayed my morning and night prayers?
3. Have I prayed with my parents and family?
4. Have I been moody and rebellious about praying and going to church on Sunday?
5. Have I asked the Holy Spirit to help me whenever I have been tempted to sin?
6. Have I asked the Holy Spirit to help me do what is right?

Responsibilities to Others

7. Have I been obedient and respectful to my parents?
8. Have I lied or been deceitful to them or to others?
9. Have I been arrogant, stubborn, or rebellious?
10. Have I talked back to parents, teachers, or other adults?
11. Have I pouted and been moody?
12. Have I been selfish toward my parents, brothers and sisters, teachers, or friends?
13. Have I hit anyone?
14. Have I held grudges or not forgiven others?
15. Have I failed to treat other children with respect; have I made fun of them and called them names?
16. Have I used bad language?
17. Have I stolen anything? If so, have I returned it?
18. Have I performed my responsibilities?
19. Have I done my homework?
20. Have I done my household chores?
21. Have I tidied up my room and my toys when asked?
22. Have I been helpful and affectionate toward my family?
23. Have I been kind and generous with my friends?

you; but stay in the city, until you are clothed with power from on high." Then he led them out as far as Bethany, and

they worshiped him, and returned to Jerusalem with great joy, and were continually in the temple blessing God.   JOHN 20:1—21:25. Now on the first day of the week Mary

lifting up his hands he blessed them. While he blessed them, he parted from them and was carried up into heaven. And

The Stations of the Cross

As a convert, ignorant of the Stations of the Cross, I found the devotion very difficult to learn. Most Stations of the Cross (also known as the Way of the Cross) books assume that you already know the basic outline of the prayer and only provide another series of meditations. While wonderful and deeply spiritual, these meditations are usually not suitable for a family setting. They are too long or too abstract.

Basically, the Stations of the Cross can be said anywhere, though in a church or at outside Stations is most customary. It would be an inspiring family devotion to make simple stations and arrange them in the home during Lent, perhaps along a hallway or around the walls of the living room. Consider using the Holy Card Shrine directions in the Crafts section of this book. To pray the Way of the Cross requires only that you meditate at each station.

A family Way of the Cross could be said every Friday afternoon (for home-schooling families), Saturday afternoon (for

school-going families), or one station each evening if that suits the children's attention span and family activities better. It can be a simple, quiet, prayerful interlude or an opportunity for conversation, sharing each other's thoughts and meditations about the station.

Before each station you say: "We adore You, O Christ, and we bless You, because by Your holy Cross, You have redeemed the world." After each station, you say an Our Father, Hail Mary, and Glory Be.

Here is a simple series of meditations for a family Stations of the Cross.

OPENING PRAYER

LORD JESUS CHRIST, take me along that holy way You once took to Your death. Take my mind, my memory, above all my reluctant heart, and let me see what once You did for love of me and all the world.

The First Station
Jesus Is Condemned to Death

Jesus is brought to stand in front of Pontius Pilate, the judge. He is innocent, but Pontius Pilate condemns Him anyway and sentences Him to death.

Prayer: It is really our bad thoughts, mean words, and angry actions that You are being punished for, Jesus. We are praying the Stations of the Cross to tell You that we are sorry for all our sins.

Our Father, Hail Mary, and Glory Be.

The Second Station
Jesus Takes His Cross

Jesus has been beaten by the soldiers. He has been laughed at and spat upon. Now He must pick up the heavy Cross and carry it while the crowd yells. He is so tired and sad, but no one seems to care.

Prayer: We care that You are tired, Jesus. We are sorry that You are sad. We would like to help You carry Your Cross with our prayers.

Our Father, Hail Mary, and Glory Be.

The Third Station
Jesus Falls the First Time

The Cross is too heavy. It is so heavy that Jesus falls down under its weight. The blood from the crown of thorns is running into His eyes, and His back aches from the scourging. People are still screaming and throwing things at Him. His heart must be as heavy as the Cross He carries.

Prayer: It is our sins that make Your Cross so heavy, Jesus. We are sorry. We love You, and we try to be good for You with our prayers and with our lives.

Our Father, Hail Mary, and Glory Be.

The Fourth Station
Jesus Meets His Blessed Mother

Suddenly, Jesus sees His Mother. She is standing at the side of the road surrounded by the crowd. Her eyes fill with tears when she sees Jesus. She wants to help Him, but she cannot. Both their hearts ache at the other's pain.

Prayer: Jesus, You and Your Blessed Mother help us whenever we ask. Our hearts ache, too, with the pain of the Stations of the Cross. We promise to pray to You and to Your Mother often, for help in our lives.

Our Father, Hail Mary, and Glory Be.

The Fifth Station
Simon of Cyrene Helps Jesus Carry the Cross

The soldiers are in a hurry. They grab Simon of Cyrene out of the crowd to carry the Cross and make Jesus go faster. Jesus was grateful to Simon for his help.

Prayer: Simon did not know he was blessed when he was carrying Your Cross—he only felt how heavy it was. Praying the Stations of the Cross will help us to re-member that carrying our crosses helps You too.

Our Father, Hail Mary, and Glory Be.

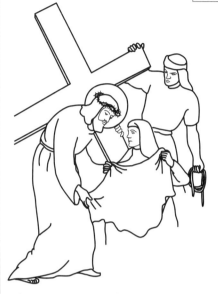

The Sixth Station
Veronica Wipes the Face of Jesus

Jesus' face is covered with sweat, blood, and dust. It is itchy and uncomfortable. In pity, Veronica runs out to the road to wipe the dirt from Jesus' face. This small act of kindness is all she can do to help Him.

Prayer: Jesus, we want to see and touch Your face, shining in glory in heaven. We know that our small acts of kindness and our prayers help us grow closer to You and Your Father in heaven.

Our Father, Hail Mary, and Glory Be.

ran, but the other disciple outran Peter and reached the tomb first; and stooping to look in, he saw the linen cloths lying there, but he did not go in. Then Simon Peter came,

where they have laid him." Peter then came out with the other disciple, and they went toward the tomb. They both

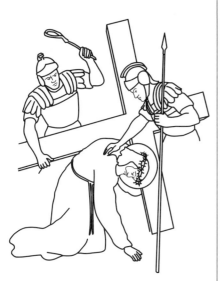

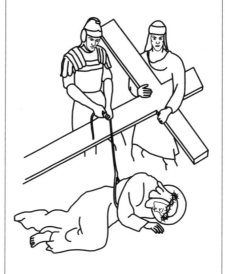

The Seventh Station
Jesus Falls the Second Time

The road is so long, and the Cross is so heavy. Exhausted, Jesus falls down again. The soldiers yell at Him and whip Him to make Him get up. Don't they know that they are hurting Him more? Jesus knows that He is suffering for the sins of the world. He gets up and keeps walking.

Prayer: Jesus, sometimes we get tired, discouraged, and impatient with the world. When we fail and fall into sin, it hurts You more. We are sorry, and we ask You to help us be as patient and brave as You.

Our Father, Hail Mary, and Glory Be.

The Eighth Station
Jesus Speaks to the Women of Jerusalem

Next, Jesus meets some of the women he taught. They are crying. They are crying for Jesus and for their own loss—what will they do without Jesus? Jesus tells them not to weep for Him, but for all the sinners of the world.

Prayer: Jesus, You told the women of Jerusalem to weep for us. Even in Your pain, You remembered us. Thank You. We will pray for sinners, too.

Our Father, Hail Mary, and Glory Be.

The Ninth Station
Christ's Third Fall

Jesus reaches the last hill before Calvary. He looks up to see how far He has to go. When he sees the hill where He knows He is going to die, His strength leaves Him, and He falls to the ground. There is still more pain, still more sorrow to endure. But Jesus loves us, so He keeps going.

Prayer: Jesus, You kept going even though You were tired, scared, and sad. You loved us then, and You love us now. We offer our prayers to tell You that we love You and want to comfort You in Your great sacrifice.

Our Father, Hail Mary, and Glory Be.

The Tenth Station
Jesus Is Stripped of His Garments

The crowd has followed Jesus and the soldiers to the top of Calvary hill. Now they laugh as the guards pull off His clothes—His robe has stuck to the blood on His back. The guards push and shove Jesus. They do not care who He is; they only see that He is an object of scorn.

Prayer: Jesus, even wounded, bleeding, roughly treated by the guards, and mocked by the crowds, You were and are still our King. We ask You to remember us in Your Kingdom.

Our Father, Hail Mary, and Glory Be.

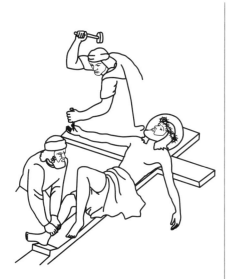

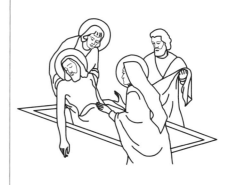

The Eleventh Station
Jesus Is Nailed to the Cross

Is this the worst? The feet that carried the message of God's Love and the hands that healed are pierced with nails as Jesus is nailed to the Cross. More wounds, more pain, and more humiliation for Jesus.

Prayer: Jesus, they tried to stop Your hands and feet from doing Your Father's work by nailing You to a Cross. You endured the pain of it for us, as You gave Your whole life for us. We thank You, and we love You.

Our Father, Hail Mary, and Glory Be.

The Twelfth Station
Jesus Dies upon the Cross

The sword that Simeon prophesied has pierced Mary's heart. The hopes of the Apostles are crushed. The veil of the Temple, symbol of the Old Covenant of God's Love, is torn in two as Jesus' death opens a New Covenant with God.

Prayer: Jesus, You spoke lovingly to everyone gathered at the foot of Your Cross. You knew the new life that Your death made possible. Speak lovingly to us when we come before You, and make us worthy of that new life in You.

Our Father, Hail Mary, and Glory Be.

The Thirteenth Station
Jesus Is Taken from the Cross

Now, all that is left is to take Jesus' body down from the Cross. All the gentleness, reverence, and love denied through this terrible day are possible now. Mary and the Apostles wonder, Is it too late? Is it over?

Prayer: Jesus, with our prayers, we join in taking Your body down from the Cross. We touch You, take the nails out, wash Your wounds, take off the crown of thorns, with love and sorrow. We grieve with Mary and want to comfort her.

Our Father, Hail Mary, and Glory Be.

The Fourteenth Station
Jesus Is Laid in the Sepulcher

Even in this time of sorrow, there is help. Joseph of Arimathea arranges for Jesus to be buried in a nearby tomb. His body is wrapped in burial cloths and sealed away. Everyone walks away, weeping. Finally, all is quiet, peaceful even.

Prayer: Jesus, we sometimes think that You are gone, that it is all over, that we will never be happy or good again. Your death and Resurrection show us that You will never leave us. We should always try to follow You with our lives and our prayers.

Our Father, Hail Mary, and Glory Be.

weeping outside the tomb, and as she wept she stooped to look into the tomb; and she saw two angels in white, sitting where the body of Jesus had lain, one at the head and one

not know the scripture, that he must rise from the dead. Then the disciples went back to their homes. But Mary stood

The Seder Meal

Haggadah means Book of Remembrance. It is the book, or liturgy, that tells the Jewish people how to celebrate the Passover *seder*, which means meal.

Christ, mysteriously both the Son of God and a faithful Jewish man, chose to use the Passover seder to institute His new meal of salvation and redemption, the Eucharist. Celebrating this seder highlights our common ancestry with our Jewish brothers and sisters and remembers the meal Jesus celebrated with his Apostles in the upper room. (See CCC 62–64, 1096, 1363–64.)

This messianic Passover meal should be celebrated on Holy Thursday. It is a wonderful close to the Lenten season and complements the Holy Thursday liturgy at your church. The meal can be eaten when the family returns from church.

The instructions for the seder meal that we give here have been adapted for Christian use. Though they seem very long and complicated, even difficult to follow, once you try them, you will see that they all lead from one lesson to another quite naturally. If you like, you can print out the various parts for everyone to say and give each participant a copy to follow.

Passover Seder Preparations

Jewish tradition and Jewish law are meticulously detailed. Every aspect of daily life and celebrations is specified. Everything supports and reinforces the belief of the Jewish people that they are set apart as God's people, the Chosen Ones. The preparations are all important to the ceremony.

Spring Cleaning!

Traditionally, the entire house, including storage areas and other non-living spaces, are meticulously cleaned to ensure that not even a crumb of leavened bread remains or is brought into the residence for the duration of the eight-day Passover holiday. Interestingly and ironically, it was this practice of cleanliness that caused the Jews to be blamed for the

bubonic plague in Europe. Their spotless and crumb-free houses were, as a result, also free of rats with their plague-carrying fleas. Jewish households, therefore, tended not to fall ill as often as their neighbors. Unjustly, they were suspected of causing the plague as revenge or punishment for persecutions.

At the very least, the kitchen and dining area should be spotless and crumb-free before your seder meal.

Table Preparations

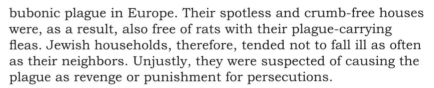

Set the table with your finest tablecloth and best dishes. In the center of the table, place:

- Floral centerpiece;
- Two taper candles and matches;
- Pitcher of ice water for drinking;
- Plate holding a small bowl of water and a washcloth, for washing;
- Wine in an easy-pour bottle or carafe (or juice as well—for the children); and a
- Large plate with several matzos (wrap the top three sheets together in a white napkin).

Set a place for each participant (plus one extra empty chair and place setting) with:

- A large dinner plate with a smaller plate on top;
- Glass for wine;
- Glass for water;
- Knife, fork, and spoon;
- Napkin (as you will see as you read further, a paper napkin would be best); and
- A cushion or pillow to sit on or lean against.

At or near the head of the table, put the Seder Plate, a plate or platter large enough to hold five small shallow bowls. Five items must be on the Seder Plate:

- Fresh parsley, one sprig for each participant, plus an extra sprig to remain on the Seder Plate;

- Horseradish, fresh sliced or pureed from a jar, about one teaspoon per participant;
- Haroset, about one tablespoon per person (recipe, page 36);
- A shank bone, or other representation of a lamb (small picture or statue of a lamb, chicken leg bone, etc.); and
- A roasted (hard-boiled) egg, plain or decorated for Easter.

In addition, place a small bowl of salt water nearby on the table.

Passover Seder Dinner Menu

After the cleaning of the home, the preparation for the Passover meal, seder, takes place. This is based on the directives given in Exodus 12. God told the Israelites the Passover shall be commemorated by eating lamb roasted over the fire, unleavened bread called matzo, and with bitter herbs, usually horseradish. There have been other elements added to the meal, including green vegetables, a roasted egg, haroset (an apple, nut and wine mixture that symbolizes the brick and the mortar that Israel's enslaved ancestors had been forced to make in Egypt), a bowl of water for washing the hands after each part of the meal, a dish of salt water, and four cups of wine.

All of the foods are placed on a special Passover plate, which is placed over the three ceremonial matzos. The matzo is placed in a linen pouch called the matzo tash. Within the matzo tash are three different sections. One piece of matzo is placed in each section, individually set apart yet united in the one container.

The meal is in two parts: the ceremonial foods: the matzo, horseradish, roasted meat, haroset, and other items, which are eaten first, and then the feasting foods: soup, lamb, or some other meat, vegetables, and dessert.

Matzo is unleavened bread, hard and crisp. It is available at some grocery stores and specialty stores. If you cannot find it, you could substitute hard crackers. The other items on both menus are easily obtained at any well-stocked grocery store:

- Gefilte fish (seasoned fish in a sausagelike casing); pickled herring, fish aspic, or any other fish appetizer could be substituted;
- Chicken soup with dumplings;
- Roast leg of lamb;
- Roast chicken;
- Roast potatoes and vegetables of your choice;
- Honey cake—a moist and dense spice cake made with honey (see one recipe on page 36).

The Messianic Passover Haggadah

Introduction

Father (or oldest man): "The Passover and Easter stories have been told for thousands of years, stories about miraculous change from misery to peace, slavery to freedom, sin to grace. One of the last things Jesus did was to celebrate Passover and retell the story to them. It is no coincidence Jesus chose the Passover meal for what the Church now celebrates as the Mass and Eucharist. God gave us the Passover celebration, and He used the same celebration to teach us even more about His love. God cared for His people, our ancestors, long ago, and He cares for His children today. Tonight we will be able to see, hear, and taste the great love God has for us!"

We Light the Candles

Father: "As we light the candles, we pray for the light of the Spirit of God to bring the special meaning of Passover and Easter to each and every one of us."

Mother (*or oldest woman; lighting the candles*): "Blessed are you, O Lord our God, King of the Universe, who has chosen each one of us out of all the people of the world and made us holy by Your Word, and in whose Name we light these celebration lights."

Father: "As the light for the celebration of redemption is lit by a woman, we remember that Jesus, our Redeemer, the promised Light of the world, came into the world through the obedience of a woman, too, who has become the Blessed Mother of us all." (*Father pours everyone a first cup of wine or juice.*)

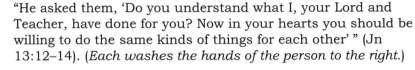

The Four Cups of Wine

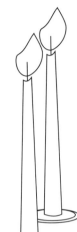

Father: "God told Moses, 'Now you will see what I will do' (Ex 6:1), and He made four promises about how He would save his people."

All:

"I will bring you out of Egypt . . .
"I will free you from slavery . . .
"I will save you by My own hand . . .
"I will take you to be My own people, and I will be your God . . ."

Father: "To remember these four promises, we drink from our cups four times."

The First Cup: The Cup of Sanctification

Father: "When Jesus joined His disciples for His last Passover supper, He knew that during that dinner He would be establishing a new covenant between God and His people. This new covenant brings redemption, sanctification, and new life to us all. Let us hold up our first cup together and bless the Lord, our God!"

All: "Blessed are you, O Lord our God, King of the Universe, who creates the fruit of the vine." (*All drink.*)

Ritual Washing of Hands

Father (*washes the hands of the person to his right and gives him the cloth and small bowl of water*): "The Scripture says only the person who has clean hands and a pure heart can stand in God's presence (Ps 24:3–4). When we wash each other's hands, we remember how Jesus, on the night of His last Passover supper, poured water into a bowl and washed the disciples' feet for them, like a servant.

"He asked them, 'Do you understand what I, your Lord and Teacher, have done for you? Now in your hearts you should be willing to do the same kinds of things for each other' " (Jn 13:12–14). (*Each washes the hands of the person to the right.*)

Parsley

Father: "Why do we celebrate Passover? God commands His people to celebrate certain special holidays every year forever."

(*Holding up the parsley*): "The Passover/Easter holidays come in the spring, when the earth turns green with new life. Only God creates life and keeps it alive. This green parsley is the sign of life."

(*Holding up the salt water*): "But while the Israelites were still slaves in Egypt, their life was miserable. The salt water stands for their tears. We know our life can be miserable and full of tears when we live in Satan's world.

"We dip our parsley in the salt water and eat it to remind us of our ancestors' tears and of how miserable our own sin makes us. We also remember how God parted the salty Red Sea to lead His people to new life."

All: "Blessed are You, O Lord our God, King of the Universe, who creates the fruit of the earth." (*All eat the dipped parsley.*)

The Four Questions

Youngest Boy (*or girl, if no sons present; standing*): "Why is this night so different from all other nights?

"On all other nights we eat leavened or unleavened bread. On this night why do we eat only unleavened bread?

"On all other nights we eat all kinds of vegetables. On this night why do we eat only bitter ones?

"On all other nights we do not dip our vegetables even once. On this night why do we dip them twice?

"On all other nights we sit on our usual seat. On this night why do we sit on soft cushions?"

The Answers

Father: "It is a special duty and a privilege to answer the four questions of Passover and tell everyone the great things God has done!"

The First Answer—The Matzo

Father: "On all other nights we eat any kind of bread, but on Passover we eat matzos, unleavened bread. When our ancestors left Egypt, they were in such a hurry they did not have time to let their dough rise. Instead, they baked it flat. The Scriptures use leaven as a symbol of sin" (see Mt 16:6, 11).

All: "Yes, just a little yeast works through the whole batch of dough. Get rid of the old yeast so that you may be like a new batch of dough without yeast—as you were created. For Messiah, our Passover lamb, has been sacrificed" (1 Cor 5:7).

Father: "During this Passover/Easter, let us break our old habits of sin and selfishness and begin fresh, new, and holy lives."

(*Holding up the plate of matzos*): "This is the bread of suffering that our ancestors ate. The three matzos in one napkin show us the special unity of the Lord God, the Messiah, and His Spirit. The Holy Trinity, three-in-one. The matzo itself is a symbol of the promised Messiah, Jesus. See how it is striped, as Jesus' back was marked by the scourging before his Crucifixion."

All: "He was wounded for our sins, bruised for our sinfulness: He suffered to bring us peace; and by His stripes our sin is healed" (Is 53:5).

Father: "See how the matzo is pierced with holes, as God's only Son was pierced by the nails and the soldier's lance."

All: "I will pour out My spirit of grace and prayer: and they will see Me whom they have pierced, and they will cry with sadness as for an only son" (Zech 12:10).

Father (*taking the middle matzo and breaking it in half*): "Just as this middle piece of the bread of suffering is broken, the Son, Jesus, also suffered. We save half for after the meal. It is wrapped in a white cloth just as Jesus' body was wrapped for burial.

(*He wraps the matzo half.*) "Children, please hide your eyes . . ."

(*Hide the matzo half somewhere in the room.*)

"Just as I have hidden the broken matzo, Jesus' body was put in a tomb, hidden for a little while. But just as the special piece of matzo will come out again to finish our celebration, Jesus rose from the dead, alive again to take us to heaven when we finish our lives. Now we share this piece of bread made with no yeast—a sign of Jesus, who has no sin and who said, 'I am the bread of life.'" (*Pass the other matzo half around the table.*)

All: "Blessed are you, O Lord our God, King of the Universe, who brings forth bread from the earth." (*All eat a piece of the matzo.*)

The Second Answer—The Maror—Bitter Herbs

Father: "On all other nights we eat all kinds of vegetables, but on Passover we eat maror, bitter ones, to remember how bitter life was for our ancestors in Egypt."

(*Holding up the horseradish*): "But the more they were oppressed, the more they multiplied and the more they spread abroad. And the Egyptians were in dread of the people of Israel. So they made the people of Israel serve with rigor, and made their lives bitter with hard service, in mortar and brick, and in all kinds of work in the field; in all their work they made them serve with rigor.

"Scoop some maror onto a piece of matzo and let the bitter taste bring tears to your eyes. Remember with compassion the tears our ancestors cried in their slavery long ago, and remember the bitterness of our own slavery to sin when we do not allow Jesus to set us free."

All: "Blessed are you, O Lord our God, King of the Universe, who has set us apart by His Word and commanded us to eat bitter herbs." (*All eat matzo with horseradish.*)

were, for fear of the Jews, Jesus came and stood among them and said to them, "Peace be with you." When he had said this, he showed them his hands and his side. Then the

these things to her. On the evening of that day, the first day of the week, the doors being shut where the disciples

The Third Answer—The Haroset—The Second Dipping

Father: "On all other nights we do not dip our vegetables even once, but tonight we dip them twice. We have already dipped the parsley in salt water."

(*Holding up the haroset*): "The Israelites worked very hard to make brick and clay to build cities for Pharaoh. We remember this in a mixture called haroset, made from apples, cinnamon, honey, ground nuts, and wine. Now again scoop some maror onto a piece of matzo, but this time, before eating it, dip it into the sweet haroset."

All: "We dip the bitter into the sweet to remember that even the most bitter things in life can be sweetened by our hope in God."

(*All eat the matzo with horseradish and sweet haroset.*)

The Fourth Answer—Tonight We Recline

Father: "On all other nights we eat sitting on regular seats, but tonight we relax on soft cushions. The first Passover was eaten in haste by a people enslaved."

All: "Once we were slaves, but now we are free!"

Father: "The Israelites were told to eat the Passover quickly, their coats ready, their walking sticks in their hands, their sandals on their feet, ready to leave the bondage of Egypt. Today we all may relax and freely enjoy the Passover seder."

All: "The Messiah said: 'Come to me, all you who labor and are heavy laden, and I will give you rest'" (Mt 11:28).

The Story of Passover

Father: "The story of Passover is a story of miracles, a story of redemption, a story of the mighty power of God to overcome evil."

Reader 1: "The Lord had promised the land of Israel to Abraham, Isaac, and Jacob. Yet here were their children living in Egypt. The Pharaoh feared them. These foreigners in our midst are prospering and have grown numerous, he

thought. Suppose they join with our enemies and turn against us! Pharaoh decided to control this foreign people, imposing harsh and bitter slavery upon the Israelites. Still, God blessed His people in strength and number."

Reader 2: "Pharaoh grew more frightened and ordered every baby boy among the Israelites to be drowned in the Nile River. One Israelite couple hid their little boy for three months. Finally, entrusting his future to God, they set him in a waterproof basket and placed him upon the river. Coming upon the basket, Pharaoh's daughter took pity on the child and chose to raise him as her own son. She called him Moses, meaning drawn from the 'water'."

Reader 3: "Moses grew to be a man. He became aware of the sufferings of his people. One day, in a rage, he killed an Egyptian who was beating a Hebrew slave. Fleeing the palace and the eye of Pharaoh, Moses became a shepherd in the land of Midian, far from the cries of his suffering brothers."

Reader 4: "The Lord, however, saw the affliction of the children of Israel and heard their prayers. He decided to raise up a deliverer to lead them out of bondage. It was then that He appeared to Moses in the midst of a bush that burned with fire, yet was not consumed. Moses listened as God told him to go to Pharaoh. Fearful and reluctant, Moses agreed to bring God's message to the king of Egypt, 'Let my people go!'"

The Second Cup: The Cup of Plagues

Father: "Moses went to Pharaoh with God's command, 'Let my people go!' But God warned Moses that Pharaoh would not easily agree. The Lord sent plagues, one by one, but with each plague, Pharaoh refused and made his heart harder against God. With the tenth and most awful plague, God broke through Pharaoh's hard heart."

All: "The Lord said, 'For I will pass through the land of Egypt that night, and I will smite all the first-born in the land of Egypt, both man and beast; and on all the gods of Egypt I will execute judgments: I am the LORD'" (Ex 12:12).

Father (*pouring cups of wine or juice for everyone*): "We fill our cups a second time now. A full cup is a sign of joy, and we are certainly filled with joy that God has set us free. But we should also remember how much that freedom cost. Many lives were lost to save our people from slavery in Egypt. But an even greater price was paid to save us from slavery to sin—the death of Jesus, God's only Son. When we say the name of each plague, dip a finger into your cup and let a drop fall onto your napkin, making the cup of joy a little less full as we remember the cost of our freedom."

All: "Blood, Frogs, Lice, Wild Animals, Cattle Disease, Boils, Hail, Locusts, Darkness, Death of the First-born!"

The Passover Lamb—The Shank Bone

Father: "In telling the Passover story, three things must be mentioned: the unleavened bread, the bitter herbs, and the Passover lamb."

All: "We have eaten the matzo to remind us how quickly our ancestors left Egypt. We have tasted the bitter herbs to remind us of the bitter life they lived there."

Father (*holding up the shank bone*): "This bone stands for the lamb whose blood on the Israelite houses was a sign to God. God told Moses, 'Your lamb shall be without blemish', and when it is killed, 'take some of the blood, and put it on the two door-posts and the lintel of the houses. . . . [E]at the flesh that night, roasted; with unleavened bread and bitter herbs. . . . In this manner you shall eat it: your loins girded, your sandals on your feet, and your staff in your hand; and you shall eat it in haste. It is the LORD's passover. . . . The blood shall be a sign for you, upon the houses where you are; and when I see the blood, I will pass over you, and no plague shall fall upon you to destroy you, when I smite the land of Egypt' (Ex 12:5, 7–8, 11). We are re- minded by Moses that it is the Lord Himself who sent the plagues, who freed our people from Egypt, and who redeemed our ancestors from slavery.

"So the Lord brought us out of Egypt with a mighty hand and an outstretched arm, with great terror and with miraculous signs and wonders (Deut 26:8).

"On that same night I will pass through Egypt . . ."

All: "I, and not an angel,"

Father: "and strike down every first-born—both men and animals—"

All: "I, and not an archangel,"

Father: "and I will bring forth judgment on all the demon gods of Egypt";

All: "I, and not a messenger,"

Father: "I am the Lord."

All: "I Myself and none other."

Father: "Since Jesus has become our perfect Passover Lamb, God has allowed the Temple in Jerusalem to be destroyed. Now no more lambs need to be sacrificed. This bone reminds us of the lamb sacrificed for the Israelites and of the Sacrifice of Jesus, the Lamb of God who takes away the sin of the world."

The Egg

Father: "Last on our seder plate is the egg. It is called hagigah, a name signifying the traditional offering brought as a symbol of mourning, reminding us of the destruction of the holy Temple in Jerusalem. The hardness of the shell also reminds us of the hardness of Pharaoh's heart—and of every heart that would not accept God's love. But the egg is also a sign of new birth and eternal life, since the shape of it shows no beginning and no end. God wants us to break the sadness and hardness of our hearts and be born into new life, ever- lasting life with Him. We will share the egg later, during the seder meal."

It Would Have Been Enough

Father: "God is so good to us! For even one little blessing we should be able to respond, Dayenu! It would have been enough!

"If the Lord had merely rescued us, but had not punished the Egyptians . . ."

All: "It would have been enough!"

Father: "If He had only destroyed their gods, but had not parted the Red Sea . . ."

All: "It would have been enough!"

Father: "If He had only destroyed our enemies, but had not fed us His food in the desert . . ."

All: "It would have been enough!"

Father: "If He had only led us through the desert, but had not given us His holy day of rest . . ."

All: "It would have been enough!"

Father: "If He had only given us His Words and Command-ments, but not a Promised Land forever . . ."

All: "It would have been enough!"

Father: "But the Holy One, the Lord, blessed be He, provided all these blessings for our ancestors. And not only these, but so many more, and so many for us, too!"

All: "Blessed are You, O God, for You have given us everything we need. You have given us Jesus our Messiah, forgiveness for sin, life with You now in our hearts, in Your Word, and in Your Eucharist, and the promise of life with You forever!"

The Third Cup: The Cup of Joy

Father: "Everyone drink the third cup now, the Cup of Joy, and we will have dinner!" (*Remove seder plate from the table. Serve the rest of the meal. Everyone feasts.*)

The Hidden Matzo

Father (*returning seder plate to the table*): "It is time to share the afikomen, the hidden matzo. Who can find it?" (*Children search for the hidden matzo, and one gives it to Father.*)

"Remember, this piece of matzo, made without leaven, is a symbol of the promised Messiah, Jesus. It was hidden, and now it is back. Jesus was buried and rose from the dead. This special matzo is the last food eaten at Passover so that its taste stays with us. It is shared the way the Passover lamb was shared from the time our ancestors were freed from Egypt until the destruction of the Temple, after Jesus' death. Jesus broke the matzo and gave thanks to the Lord."

All: "Blessed are You, O God, King of the Universe, who brings forth bread from the earth."

Father (*breaking the matzo into pieces*): "It was here that Jesus added the words: "This is my body, which is given for you. Do this in remembrance of me" (Lk 22:19). Jesus changed the significance of the matzo forever and gives us His Body at every Holy Mass. The matzo, like the Eucharist, is broken in small pieces and everyone must eat his own piece, just as each of us must accept Jesus' grace for ourselves. No other person can do it for us.

"Think about Jesus, the Lamb of God, Whose Body we are privileged truly to receive in the Eucharist, our once and forever Passover sacrifice. Eat this piece of matzo now, and let its taste stay with you." (*All eat.*)

The Prophet Elijah

Father (*lifting the cup from the empty place at the table*): "This cup is the cup of Elijah the Prophet. Elijah did not see death, but was taken up to heaven alive in a mighty wind riding a fiery chariot. Our ancestors and the Jewish people everywhere hoped that Elijah would come at Passover to announce the coming of the Messiah.

"Before the birth of John the Baptist, an angel of the Lord said, 'And he will go on before [the Lord,] in the spirit and power of Elijah . . . to make ready for the Lord a people prepared' (Lk 1:17).

"Later Jesus said about John, 'He is Elijah who is to come' (Mt 11:14).

"It was this same John who saw Jesus and announced, 'Behold, the Lamb of God, who takes away the sin of the world!' (Jn 1:29).

"The extra cup also reminds us to pray for our spiritual brothers, those Jews still seeking the Messiah, who has already come to them and who waits longingly for them. The empty chair reminds us, and every household observing Passover tonight, that there are still those who are persecuted for their faith or who have not yet discovered the great love of God. We pray that someday soon all may freely rejoice in the majesty of God everywhere in the world. Someone open the door to welcome the Prophet of God to our seder!"

(*Someone gets up to open the door. You may leave it open or ajar if you wish.*)

The Fourth Cup: The Cup of Promise

Father: "Remember God's promise, 'I will take you for my people, and I will be your God' (Ex 6:7). Now let us fill our cups for the fourth and last time and give thanks to our great God. Give thanks to the Lord, for He is good."

All: "His love lasts forever."

Father: "Give thanks to the Lord, God of all creation."

All: "His love lasts forever."

Father: "Give thanks to Him who destroyed the demon gods of Egypt."

All: "His love lasts forever."

Father: "Give thanks to Him who destroys the works of Satan today."

All: "His love lasts forever."

Father: "Give thanks to Him who saved Israel from slavery in Egypt."

All: "His love lasts forever."

Father: "Give thanks to Him who saves us from slavery to sin."

All: "His love lasts forever.'

Father: "Give thanks to God, our God, who chose us to be His people."

All: "His love lasts forever."

Father: "Lift your cups and bless the Lord!"

All: "Blessed are you, O Lord our God, King of the Universe, who creates the fruit of the vine." (*All drink.*)

Father: "Our Passover celebration is complete, just as God's plan for our salvation through Jesus is complete. Now it is up to us to go and live His Word. Let us wish each other peace."

All: "Peace!"

Haroset

Ingredients

- 4 large firm apples, peeled, cored, and finely chopped
- 2 cups finely chopped walnuts
- 2 teaspoons white sugar
- 2 teaspoons ground cinnamon
- 2 teaspoons lemon zest (optional)
- ¼ cup sweet red wine or apple juice

Directions

Mix apples, nuts, sugar, and cinnamon together in a bowl. Add enough wine or juice to make a smooth mixture and mix in to blend thoroughly.

You may chop the apple and walnuts and mix the haroset in a food processor. Be careful not to overprocess it, though; it should retain a slightly rough texture.

Keep the haroset in refrigerator covered for up to two weeks.

Honey Cake

Ingredients

- 3 cups all-purpose flour
- 1 cup honey
- 1 teaspoon baking soda
- 1 teaspoon baking powder
- 1 teaspoon cinnamon
- ¼ teaspoon salt
- ½ cup strong, cold coffee
- grated rind and juice of 1 orange
- 1 teaspoon vanilla
- 2 tablespoons butter, softened
- 1 cup white sugar
- 4 eggs, separated
- 1 cup chopped walnuts

Directions

Grease and flour a 10-inch tube pan or two 9-inch round cake pans. Preheat the oven to 325°F.

Bring the honey to a boil in a small saucepan on the stove or in a glass bowl in the microwave. Set it aside to cool.

Sift or mix the flour with the dry ingredients. Combine the coffee with the orange rind, juice, and vanilla.

Cream the butter with the sugar, then mix in the honey. Beat the egg yolks until they are light and blend them into the honey mixture.

Add half the flour to the honey and egg yolk mixture and mix it in. Add half the coffee mixture to the batter, mixing well. Add the remaining flour and the remaining coffee, mixing well between additions. Stir in the nuts.

Beat the egg whites until stiff and gently fold them into the batter. Spoon the batter into the prepared pans and bake for about 50 minutes. Cool the cake in the pan for about 10 minutes, then remove the cake from the pan and allow to cool completely on a cake rack.

Decorate with a light dusting of icing sugar.

The Light of the World: Making a Paschal Candle

A Paschal candle can enrich your family's observance of the Easter season by bringing the "light of the world" into your home in a concrete way. (See CCC 638, 647–55.) The candle should have a place of honor in your home, on a family prayer altar, or on the table for all meals, replacing the palms that lie there during Holy Week.

This "home Paschal candle" is a reminder of the large Paschal candle that is in Catholic churches throughout the world from the beginning of the Easter Vigil until after Evening Prayer on Pentecost Sunday, fifty days later. On the night of Holy Saturday, at the beginning of the Easter Vigil, the Paschal candle is blessed and then lit from a new fire, which symbolizes the Resurrection. This large candle is carried in procession to the altar. The priest or deacon sings, "The Light of Christ", and all the people answer, "Thanks be to God". Placed on a high stand, this candle symbolizes Christ, the Light of the World. It is used for its Resurrection symbolism at baptisms and funerals.

Fortunately a Paschal candle is quite easy to make. If you make one, try to attend the Easter Vigil and bring home the blessed fire (you can get it from the Paschal candle at church after Mass by lighting a candle from its flame) to light your candle with. You can also do this on Easter morning.

(To carry the flame home safely, used melted wax to stick a candle in a tall glass jar. Light this candle with a taper and, when home, light your Paschal candle from it. To reduce the risk of burned fingers or a fire, place the candle jar upright inside another, larger, fireproof container partially filled with some non-flammable material such as sand, rice, dried beans, or potting soil. Push the jar well down into this material for stability.)

What You Need

- Start with a tall pillar candle. Try to find a liturgical candle of more than 51 percent beeswax in a religious goods store, or make your own.

- Oil paint of various colors, especially red. Shapes can be carved into the candle and then painted.

- Paper pictures to be stuck in place with melted wax, small beads, glass-headed pins, sequins, or colored eggshell pieces to create mosaiclike pictures.

Decorating the Candle

The candle is decorated with symbols, beginning with a cross embellished with the date, and the Greek letters alpha and omega. The alpha and omega are placed above and below the vertical bar of the cross, and the numerals fit in the four corners around the center, as shown in the illustration on this page. The cross, date, and alpha and omega emphasize the words said by the priest at the Easter Vigil: "Christ yesterday and today, the beginning and the end" and "all time belongs to him and all the ages, to him be glory and power through every age for ever. Amen."

Next, you may add other symbols of redemption and resurrection, such as: the lamb with a victory banner, dolphin (ancient symbol of redemption), grapes and wheat, peacock (the glorious life of resurrection is represented in the glorious fantail of the peacock).

Finally, you will place incense at the four ends of the lines that form the cross and at its center with the prayer, "By His holy and glorious wounds, may Christ our Lord guard us and keep us. Amen." Use cloves for their fragrance and because they look like nails. Poke the candle with a hot skewer, then insert the clove. (Even though the cloves are for decoration on the candle and are not burned, they are symbolic of incense.)

When the candle is decorated and everyone is satisfied, ask your priest to bless it.

May it light your Easter celebration!

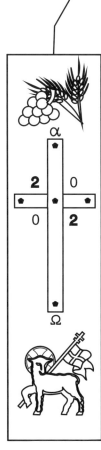

A Garden for Mary

Planning a garden is, in many ways, like decorating the interior of your house. Both contribute to imparting a sense of beauty to your domestic church, and this beauty in turn teaches and reassures the family of the Beauty of God.

Both your home and your garden should be practical, attractive living spaces that suit your family. Three major factors govern the arrangement of both inside and outside the home: the area, the intended use of the space, and your own personal taste. In other words, what you have, what you need, and what you like.

Unlike a house, garden design changes from one week to the next. Plants grow, bloom, and die back; sunlight moves across the area; seasons come and go. For many, this element of change and surprise is the main appeal of gardening. Certain plants may be quite spectacular in one season yet unobtrusive in others. Color schemes, views, and density can change from season to season, too. It all gives glory to God, to His great plan and His marvelous creation.

So, attractive and well-kept gardens surrounding your house express your appreciation for the gifts God has given you. In case this has just increased your garden-guilt to unbearable levels, let me assure you that gardens need not be expensive, time-consuming, or elaborate. A collection of perennials (gathered from friends and relatives who are dividing theirs) needs very little maintenance and looks better every year. Adding annuals to brighten the edges finishes a garden off nicely.

A Mary Garden

I have reserved one special corner of our front garden (where a pile of rocks too big to move makes a jumbled grotto-like space) to make a Mary Garden. A Mary Garden is one that is designed to honor Mary with both its arrangement and the choice of flowers. It can include a statue or small shrine to Mary. Some Mary Gardens have stepping-stones laid out in the form of a rosary winding through the plants. Mary Gardens are a simple and beautiful devotion, an act of faith with a long history in Europe.

Our Mary Garden is in a quiet corner of the front yard, in a spot that is easily seen from the windows and by visitors. I have already planted my Mary Garden corner with lots of narcissus and daffodils, recycled from forcing in the house for Easter. Several lilac bushes form a backdrop for the rocks. Columbine and lily of the valley bloom yearly, and I plant marigolds and morning glories in the spring. A small concrete statue of our Lady will be added this year, and flowers planted around her feet. I plan to add a bench for quiet moments of contemplation in the future.

Early spring (just after Easter, in fact) is the perfect time to begin planning your Mary Garden and starting seeds for later transplanting. There is a long history of honoring Mary with flowers, and in this tradition many flowers were named after the Blessed Virgin in medieval times. All are almost as beautiful as Mary herself and appropriate for a Mary Garden.

Always remembering that gardening should be enjoyable as well as creative, consider starting your Mary Garden with annual plants (annual plants last for one growing season and then die over the winter) either started from seed yourself or purchased from a local nursery. There is usually a wide variety of inexpensive annuals available at nurseries; for your Mary Garden try to choose mostly blue and white flowers, like alyssum, pansies, and petunias.

Depending on your time and budget, you can start with some perennials (plants which overwinter and may spread every year—they are initially more expensive than annuals) or add them one at a time as your Mary Garden develops. The beauty and fragrance of roses are a natural addition to a garden dedicated to our Blessed Mother. Peonies are as fragrant and beautiful as roses but usually not so difficult to grow, provided you don't transplant them. Daylilies, while not the same kind of lilies as those associated with Mary and other virgin saints, are reliable and attractive, as are lilies of the valley. Clematis, also known as Virgin's bower, is a perennial climbing plant with blue, purple, or white flowers, a good choice for an arbor or trellis.

How Flowers Got Their Scent

(An apocryphal tale.)

It is said that all the flowers in the world lost their scent when Adam and Eve disobeyed God and were exiled from the Garden of Eden. Flowers were still beautiful to behold, bees and birds still flew around them, but they had no pleasant fragrance to fill the summer air and no perfume to scent a winter evening.

Of course, since all the people born of Adam and Eve had never smelled a flower's beautiful scent, no one knew what he was missing and no one noticed the lack. Abraham, Jacob, Moses, David, Daniel, all through the history of God's people—no one ever thought to wish for the perfume of a flower.

And with so many things happening in the land of Israel, no wonder. There were wars and famines, conquering armies and terrible storms, cities to build and fields to plow, children to raise and grandchildren to teach, stories to tell and songs to learn. Then, most amazing of all, there came a great Teacher.

His name was Jesus, and He was the Son of God come to redeem God's people for the disobedience of Adam and Eve.

But this story isn't about Jesus; it's about His Blessed Mother, Mary. Now Mary, being the Mother of Jesus, was conceived and born without the sin of Adam and Eve on her soul. She was obedient where Adam and Eve had been disobedient; she was kind and gentle, patient and humble. Everyone loved her.

Even after Jesus returned to His Father in heaven, His Apostles and disciples looked after His Mother and tried to follow her example of love. When it was time for the Virgin Mary to die, all the Apostles were there in the house with her, except Thomas. Poor Thomas, he had missed the first appearance of Jesus after the Resurrection, and then he missed saying good-bye to our Blessed Mother.

Thomas knew that Mary was dying, and he traveled hard all through the night. When he arrived at Mary's house the next morning, he was grief-stricken to hear that he was too late. All the apostles tried to comfort him. But Thomas would not be comforted, and he begged to see her face one last time.

So the apostles took him to the tomb where they had laid Mary's body the night before. With great effort, they moved the stone aside. To their amazement a beautiful fragrance wafted from the tomb.

When they looked into the tomb, where Mary's body had been, they saw only a mound of beautiful flowers. Flowers that had regained their scent.

Lord!" When Simon Peter heard that it was the Lord, he put on his clothes, for he was stripped for work, and sprang into the sea. But the other disciples came in the boat,

now they were not able to haul it in, for the quantity of fish. That disciple whom Jesus loved said to Peter, "It is the

Pentecost—The Red-Hot Celebration

After Christ ascended to His Father (on what we celebrate as Ascension Day), He sent the Holy Spirit to comfort and guide His Apostles. This day, on which we celebrate the descent of the Holy Spirit, is called Pentecost.

The festival taking place at the time of the descent of the Holy Spirit was the Old Testament Feast of Weeks, the celebration of the first fruits of the harvest. This festival was held seven weeks after Passover. You can read about the Feast of Weeks in Deuteronomy 16:9–12 and about Pentecost in the Acts of the Apostles, chapter 2. On the first Pentecost feast of the New Covenant, seven weeks after Easter, the Church received the fruits and gifts of the Holy Spirit. (See CCC 659, 731–32, 857.)

The intense love and fire of the Holy Spirit are represented in the use of red as the liturgical color for Pentecost Sunday. As a consequence, fiery hot food, food cooked over flames, and red food seem appropriate for a Pentecost feast!

Here is a red-hot salad you can include in your meal:

Red-Hot Jello

Ingredients
- 2 cups boiling water
- ⅔ cup cinnamon candies
- 2 3-ounce packages red gelatin mix
- 2 cups applesauce

Directions
- Add candies to boiling water, and stir until dissolved.
- Add gelatin mix, and stir until dissolved.
- Add applesauce to gelatin mixture, and pour into mold or serving dish(es).
- Chill for several hours until firm.

Twelve-Fruit Salad

The twelve Fruits of the Holy Spirit are: charity, joy, peace, patience, kindness, goodness, generosity, gentleness, faithfulness, modesty, self-control, and chastity (see CCC 1830–32). Have a twelve-fruit salad and Holy Spirit cookies for Pentecost dinner!

Ingredients
- 1 3-ounce package red gelatin mix, prepared
- 1 container whipped topping
- 12 different fruits

Fruits to consider: grapes, oranges, peaches, strawberries, blueberries, raspberries, blackberries, apples, kiwi, canned pineapple, pears, cherries, tangerines, apricots.

Directions
- Allow the gelatin to set partially, just to the consistency of soft pudding.
- Stir the gelatin into the whipped topping thoroughly.
- Wash fruit and slice into bite-sized pieces; fold into flavored whipped topping.
- Chill for several hours and serve.

Holy Spirit Cookies

Finish your dinner or picnic with some sweet treats. Using slice-and-bake sugar cookies or your own homemade cookies, decorate them with red toppings and symbols of the Holy Spirit.

Give the older children the task of making little circular templates out of stiff paper. Cut out the shapes of a flame, cross, beam of light, and descending dove from the center of each template. (See CCC 696, 701.) Frost cookies with prepared or homemade white frosting. Lay the templates on top and moisten frosting slightly, then sprinkle red sugar liberally over stencil. Carefully brush sugar off the stencil and lift it off the cookie.

Now go forth and make disciples of all nations!

Saints of the Season

Celebrating Feast Days

Even in the midst of Lent, we have much to celebrate in our faith. In a sense, it is an honor, joy, and privilege to be able to practice penitential acts. We are blessed and give thanks that they are effective, that through these practices we express repentance and grow closer to God.

Sometimes, though, the celebration needs to be a bit more overt than a prayer of thanksgiving. If we do not celebrate with food, gatherings, songs, parades, and special decorations, we soon lose sight of what it is we have to be thankful for (and what we need to have repentance for as well). Our joyous faith can disappear into the duties of the day-to-day and the secular tug of the workplace. Celebrate it or lose it, you might say.

Of course, every Mass is both a celebration and a reparation. But the Church also gives us feast days, seasons of celebration and seasons of penance. Even during the great seasons of Christmas and Easter and sprinkled throughout ordinary time are smaller feasts, the feast days of the saints. Celebrating feast days brings this liturgical life of the Church into the life of the family and helps build and strengthen the domestic church.

The saints are our heroes. They are not simply those to whom we can pray for help or see as (perhaps daunting) examples of holy lives. They are real heroes who can inspire and instruct us in our own lives. We have the heroic examples of the Apostles, who were for the most part simple fishermen, led by the Holy Spirit to build a new world. Then there were the early Christian martyrs, who defied the Roman Empire and clung to their faith. Saints and martyrs throughout history who have taught the faith, spoken the truth, and served God with their lives are true heroes too. Learning about a particular life of faith can inspire us to model our lives after it. (See CCC 2030 and 2683.)

The communion of saints is an invaluable resource to us, a source of intercession, help, and inspiration. Every struggle we face is shared by a saint. Every trial we encounter has been fought and won before by one of our brothers or

sisters in Christ. Each saint has a unique story, some particular strength that he can bring to your family.

In children's minds, celebration means food. After all, feast days would not be feast days unless we were meant to feast and be jolly. A special meal, something that relates to the life of the saint, is a central part of a feast-day celebration. (For example, on the feast day of Saint Peter, I serve fresh fish: "Come and I will make you a fisher of men.") So, on Pentecost add sparklers to a cake to symbolize the flames of the Holy Spirit, or hold your celebration outdoors with candle lanterns, a bonfire, and fireworks.

Celebration also means preparation, and it is important to prepare for these celebrations. We use all of Advent to prepare for Christmas and all of Lent to prepare for Easter in order to be wholehearted in our anticipation and celebration of the feast days. A period of preparation helps us celebrate a saint's feast day wholeheartedly and helps the whole family participate in honoring the saint. Three days is usually sufficient to cook, organize, perhaps attend Mass and go to confession, and, most importantly, to include the saint in the family's prayers. It is important not to forget to pray for the intercession of the saint you are celebrating. The Liturgy of the Hours or an old missal frequently has beautiful prayers to use, or you could make up your own. (See CCC 1174–75.)

Sometimes, the preparation can be fairly elaborate—you can invite friends and family to join and plan a special menu including foods from the saint's native country or patronage country. Other times, when the date just sort of sneaks up on you, a quick cake and some imaginative decoration will make an impromptu party in no time.

Many saints have acquired symbols over the years, objects and images that represent some part of their story, and these are frequently shown in their portraits. Used in the celebrations, these symbols help teach us about the saints and their place in the life of the Church and our lives. The symbols and the lives of the saints also help in creating the celebration, suggesting themes, possible menus, and activities.

Collecting some theme-decorations and keeping them in a special place will help the preparation and the decorating. Some colored candles, streamers, symbols for the saints, and maybe some specially shaped cake pans, collected over the years, will really help putting together a feast-day celebration. We decorate our homes for Christmas and Easter. Our churches are made beautiful year round for the greater glory of God, so why not something for feast days as well?

A banner reserved just for these special occasions helps make feast days a stronger tradition. A banner does not have to be ornate or detailed. It is just a simple wall hanging. A saints' day banner could include a crown, because the saints are crowned in heaven, flames for the Holy Spirit, and the words "Saints in Heaven, Pray for Us". The symbols of the name-saints of your family could be added to the banner as well. (For more about making banners, see the Crafts section of this book.)

Celebration also means teaching. Celebrating a slight variation of feast days for name days marks in some special way the feast day of the saint whose name is used as a baptismal or confirmation name. Canon law specifies that each baptismal name should contain a saint's name. In some places the custom of choosing a different name for confirmation is not as common as it seems to have been twenty or thirty years ago. If a child does not have a special confirmation name, he could choose a patron for whom he feels a special affinity.

In celebrating a name saint, we also celebrate the life of the child. We teach the children that they, too, are special in the eyes of God and loved by both family and God. In a very significant way, our names not only define who we are, they define our existence. Name days celebrate both the feast day of the saint and the special place that child holds for a member of the communion of saints.

For the children, and I must confess for myself as well, the idea of having a patron saint in heaven interceding for me to our Lord and watching out for me is a very comforting and sort of com-

panionable idea. We each have a guardian angel, of course, but also to have a patron saint who understands the difficulties of being human is a very special gift.

At first, celebrating feast days and especially name days may seem fairly frivolous, perhaps just an excuse for another birthday party. It seems to me that it really is an opportunity to enrich family life by threading it through with the strength of the communion of saints and the liturgical life of the Church.

The following pages give a brief outline of the lives of three saints (Saint Patrick, Saint Joseph, Saint George) whose feast days fall in March and April and a brief description of the Feast of the Annunciation. We then suggest a few ways to celebrate these feasts in your family. These feast days offer a brief respite from the somber character of Lent and remind us of how much we have to celebrate in our faith.

The saints were heroic in their practice of faith, hope, and love. The following prayers can help your family cultivate these virtues too.

An Act of Faith

    O God,
    I firmly believe all the truths that You have revealed
    And that You teach us through Your Church,
    For You are Truth itself
    And can neither deceive nor be deceived.

An Act of Hope

    O God,
    I hope with complete trust that You will give me,
    Through the merits of Jesus Christ,
    All necessary grace in this world
    And everlasting life in the world to come,
    For this is what You have promised,
    And You always keep Your promises.

An Act of Love

    O God,
    I love You with my whole heart above all things,
    Because You are infinitely good:
    And for Your sake I love my neighbor as I love myself.

Saint Patrick

Bishop, Apostle of Ireland
Patron of Ireland
Feast day: March 17
Saint Patrick's symbols: cross, harp, serpent, baptismal font, and the shamrock

The Life of the Saint

Saint Patrick of Ireland is one of the world's most popular saints. Along with Saint Nicholas (Santa Claus) and Saint Valentine, Saint Patrick's feast day is celebrated, or at least recognized, by many Christians throughout the world. There are many legends and stories about the life and works of Saint Patrick.

Patrick was born around 385 of Roman parents. His father had a position in the Roman government of the British territory. At sixteen, he was captured during a raid and taken to Ireland, a land of Druids and pagans. For six years he lived in slavery, tending sheep alone on the hills. During his captivity he learned the language and practices of the Irish people.

Though Patrick was probably raised as a Christian, he was quite ignorant of his Christian faith. During his captivity, he turned to God in prayer. He wrote: "More and more my love of God and reverence for him began to increase. My faith grew stronger and my zeal so intense that in the course of a single day I would say as many as a hundred prayers, and almost as many in the night. Even in times of snow or frost or rain I would rise before dawn to pray. I never felt the worse for it" (from Joseph Duffy, *Patrick in His Own Words* (Dublin: Veritas, 1972).

Patrick's captivity lasted until he was twenty-two. At that time, he was instructed in a dream, "Look, your ship is ready." From this he understood that he was to walk to the coast and return home. He walked two hundred miles to the coast, where he found a ship preparing to sail. After some reluctance from the sailors, he was permitted to board, and he sailed to Gaul, and then traveled to Britain, where he was welcomed by relatives.

The journey had been long and difficult. At one point, he and his traveling companions had no food. They mocked his Christianity and asked, "Why does your God not help you, if He is so great and powerful?" Patrick replied with confidence that the Lord would help them all. Soon after, they came across a herd of wild pigs and had a feast that lasted for two days. Some time after he finally returned to the arms of his family, he had another dream in which the people of Ireland were calling out to him, "We ask you, boy, come and walk once more among us."

Convinced that he was not ready to take on such a task, he began to prepare himself for it. He began studies for the priesthood and was ordained by Saint Germanus, the Bishop of Auxerre, with whom he studied for years. Later, Patrick was ordained a bishop and was sent to take the gospel to Ireland. Pope Celestine I had originally assigned Palladius to the task, but he, through fear or death (accounts vary on this point), was unable to carry out his instructions. Saint Germanus then recommended his student Patrick to the Pope.

He arrived in Ireland on March 25, 433, at Slane. One legend says that upon landing he met a chieftain of one of the tribes, who tried to kill Patrick. Patrick converted Dichu (the chieftain) after Dichu found he was unable to move his arm until he became friendly with Patrick.

Patrick began preaching the gospel throughout Ireland, converting many. He defeated all who were sent against him, overthrew or banished the priests of pagan religions, survived many persecutions, and fearlessly and joyfully went wherever he was needed to spread God's Word. He and his disciples preached and converted thousands and built churches all over the country. Kings, their families, and entire kingdoms converted to Christianity upon hearing Patrick's message.

According to a famous legend, on one occasion Saint Patrick picked a shamrock to explain to the king and assembled chieftains, by its triple leaf and single stem, the great doctrine of the Blessed Trinity. As a result of Saint Patrick's teaching, the Ard-Righ (High King) granted permission to Patrick to preach the faith throughout the length and breadth of Ireland.

Patrick preached and converted the people of Ireland for around thirty years. He would stay in an area just long enough to plant the seeds of a church, then move on.

By the end of his life, Ireland was almost completely Christian. He worked many miracles and wrote of his love for God in his *Confessions*. After years of living in poverty, traveling, and enduring much suffering, he died March 17, 461 (although this date is not certain).

Celebrating the Feast Day

Instead of oceans of green beer and mountains of potato dishes, a family celebration should focus on the symbolism of shamrocks, snakes, and the cross. Remember to add prayers asking for the aid and intercession of Saint Patrick to your family prayers.

Read the life of the saint out loud, either from this book or from the many other excellent lives of the saints available in bookstores, libraries, or on-line. Explain Saint Patrick's trust in God and love of prayer.

Place a large shamrock at the foot of the family crucifix, and retell in your own words Saint Patrick's story of the shamrock: that three distinct leaves join together to make one leaf. Each is a separate individual; each is essential to the whole. As illustration use a potted shamrock; these are often available for sale in flower shops and grocery stores at this time of year. Making shamrocks from three green construction paper heart shapes is an easy craft for young children.

Explain that Saint Patrick did not actually drive all the snakes off the island of Ireland—like some exterminator on contract from heaven—but that snakes represent the evils of paganism. Saint Patrick did drive Druidism, paganism, and other evils out of Ireland, replacing them with the love and mercy of the Christian faith.

A game of Snakes and Ladders (also known as Chutes and Ladders) can be a vivid way to teach this lesson. The ladders of faith and the snakes of error fill our lives, and it takes a steady gaze to the goal of heaven to guide us safely through.

Unless the feast falls on a Friday, shepherd's pie would be an appropriate (and Lenten simple) meal for a Saint Patrick's Day celebration, in commemoration of the years the saint spent as a slave-shepherd to his Irish captors and of Christ, the Good Shepherd of us all. Irish soda bread is also appropriate for this feast.

(This he said to show by what death he was to glorify God.) And after this he said to him, "Follow me." Peter turned and saw following them the disciple whom Jesus loved,

you are old, you will stretch out your hands, and another will gird you and carry you where you do not wish to go."

Shepherd's Pie

Ingredients

- 4 tablespoons butter
- 1 medium onion, finely chopped
- 1 large clove garlic, chopped
- 3 stalks celery, finely chopped (optional)
- 3 medium carrots, sliced or diced (optional)
- 3 cups cooked lamb or beef
- 2 tablespoons flour
- ¾ cup beef or chicken broth (water or bouillon cubes dissolved in water may be used)
- 1 teaspoon rosemary, savory, or thyme, to your preference
- Salt and pepper to taste
- 1 cup frozen peas (optional)
- 3 cups cooked, mashed potatoes (fairly soft, with added milk)

Directions

Preheat oven to 375°F.

Brown the onion in the butter in a skillet. When it is transparent, add the garlic (and finely chopped celery and carrots, if you wish). When the vegetables are browned, add the meat and stir until it is well combined.

Sprinkle the flour over the meat mixture, and stir until it is evenly distributed. Let it brown for a few minutes. Slowly add the broth, stirring well as the gravy thickens. Add the herbs, and salt and pepper to taste. You may add frozen peas now too, if you wish.

Spoon the meat and gravy into a 1½-quart casserole, deep pie dish, or cast-iron skillet.

Spread the mashed potatoes over the top, and cover evenly to the edge of the dish. Make a crisscross design on the potatoes with a fork, or a rough hilly surface with the back of a spoon.

Bake the shepherd's pie for 35 to 40 minutes, or until the meat is bubbling hot and the potatoes are browned. The vegetables, if used, will finish cooking in the oven too.

Serve with Irish soda bread and a cabbage salad.

Irish Soda Bread

Ingredients

- 3 cups flour
- 2 teaspoons baking powder
- 1 teaspoon baking soda
- ½ teaspoon salt
- ¾ cup cold butter
- 2 cups raisins, preferably golden
- 1 egg
- ½ cup honey
- 1 cup buttermilk (or ⅞ cup milk with 2 tablespoons lemon juice or vinegar added)

Directions

Preheat oven to 350°F, and butter a heavy skillet or casserole (10 to 11 inches in diameter and at least 2 to 3 inches deep). Cast iron is best.

Sift the flour, baking powder, soda, and salt into a large mixing bowl. Cut the butter into small pieces and add. Mix it into the flour with a pastry blender or two knives or your fingers until the mixture is fine and crumbly. Add the raisins and stir to distribute evenly.

Beat the egg in another bowl until frothy. Beat in the honey, then the buttermilk.

Gradually blend the liquids into the flour, stirring gently with a fork, until the mixture is evenly moistened but not smooth. It should be rough and lumpy.

Spoon the batter into the prepared pan, and spread it to fill the pan. It can mound in the middle. Bake at 350°F for about an hour or until the middle is set.

Cut into wedges and serve warm from the pan with butter and honey. Serves 8 to 12, fewer if they are teen-aged boys.

Prayer: *Lorica (or Breastplate) of Saint Patrick*

I arise today
Through a mighty strength, the invocation of the Trinity,
Through a belief in the Threeness,
Through confession of the Oneness
Of the Creator of creation.

I arise today
Through the strength of Christ's birth and His baptism,
Through the strength of His Crucifixion and His burial,
Through the strength of His Resurrection and His Ascension,
Through the strength of His descent for the judgment of doom.

I arise today
Through the strength of the love of cherubim,
In obedience of angels,
In service of archangels,
In the hope of resurrection to meet with reward,
In the prayers of patriarchs,
In preachings of the Apostles,
In faiths of confessors,
In innocence of virgins,
In deeds of righteous men.

I arise today
Through the strength of heaven;
Light of the sun, Splendor of fire, Speed of lightning,
Swiftness of the wind, Depth of the sea, Stability of the earth,
Firmness of the rock.

I arise today
Through God's strength to pilot me;
God's might to uphold me,
God's wisdom to guide me,
God's eye to look before me,
God's ear to hear me,
God's word to speak for me,
God's hand to guard me,
God's way to lie before me,
God's shield to protect me,
God's hosts to save me
From snares of the devil,
From temptations of vices,

From every one who desires me ill,
Afar and anear,
Alone or in a multitude.

I summon today all these powers between me and evil,
Against every cruel merciless power that opposes my body and soul,
Against incantations of false prophets,
Against black laws of pagandom,
Against false laws of heretics,
Against craft of idolatry,
Against spells of women and smiths and wizards,
Against every knowledge that corrupts man's body and soul.
Christ shield me today
Against poison, against burning,
Against drowning, against wounding,
So that reward may come to me in abundance.

Christ with me,
Christ before me,
Christ behind me,
Christ in me,
Christ beneath me,
Christ above me,
Christ on my right,
Christ on my left,
Christ when I lie down,
Christ when I sit down,
Christ in the heart of every man who thinks of me,
Christ in the mouth of every man who speaks of me,
Christ in the eye that sees me,
Christ in the ear that hears me.

I arise today
Through a mighty strength, the invocation of the Trinity,
Through a belief in the Threeness,
Through a confession of the Oneness
Of the Creator of creation.

—Saint Patrick (ca. 377)

Saint Joseph

Husband of Mary
Patron of the Universal Church, Patron of Belgium, Canada,
    China, and Peru, of workers, fathers, the poor, craftsmen, and
    of a happy death
Feast day: March 19
Saint Joseph's symbols: Infant Jesus, monstrance, chalice,
    cross, lamb, Bible, ladder, tools, dove, lily, plane, carpenter's
    square

The Life of the Saint

Saint Joseph, the spouse of the Blessed Virgin Mary and foster father of our Blessed Lord, was a descendant of King David. This fulfilled the Scripture prophecy that the Messiah would come from "the house of David". Of all the men in the world throughout history, a simple village carpenter named Joseph was the one chosen to help raise the Child Jesus to adulthood. To his faithful, loving care were entrusted the childhood and youth of the Redeemer of the world. The Bible tells us that he was a just man (Mt 1:19). That means he was a good man, honest, fair, and God-loving.

After an angel told Mary that she would be the Mother of God, Saint Joseph wondered what to do. An angel appeared to him in a dream and told him not to worry, that the child was the Messiah conceived by the Holy Spirit. Joseph was to be her husband and protect the Child as He grew (Mt 1:20–21). Joseph decided to trust the angel and God. He married Mary and took her into his home.

After Jesus was born in Bethlehem, the angel appeared to Joseph a second time, warning him that the Child was in danger (Mt 2:13). Again, Joseph obeyed the angel's message and took his family to Egypt to escape from Herod's soldiers. After a time, the Holy Family, again following the instructions of an angel, returned to their home village of Nazareth (Mt 2:20–23).

Not much else is known about Saint Joseph. But we are sure that he must have been a good and honorable man to be so favored by God. After the Mother of God herself, no one has ever been so blessed with virtues as Saint Joseph. In purity of heart, in chastity of life, in humility, patience, fortitude, gentleness, and manliness of character, he shows us the perfect model of the true Christian.

The only other story in the Bible that mentions Saint Joseph is the episode in which Jesus was missing for three days (Lk 2:41–51). Finally Joseph and Mary found Him in the Temple teaching the scribes and elders. Imagine how worried Joseph must have been! God had told him to look after the Child. Saint Joseph must have felt that he had not done a very good job. When they found Him, Mary and Joseph scolded Him a little and returned home to Nazareth. Jesus returned home with Mary and Joseph and after this "was subject to them". That means he was obedient and respectful of their parental authority.

As was the custom of the time, Saint Joseph was probably older than Mary, though this, like many other details of his life, is not clear. He probably died before Jesus began his ministry in his thirties.

A model for fathers, Saint Joseph is invoked as a protector of the family. A carpenter by trade, he has been declared the patron saint of all working people, of craftsmen, and of the poor. He is the model of a perfect Christian life and the patron of a happy death. His patronage also extends over the Mystical Body of Christ, over the Christian family, the Christian school, and all individuals who appeal to his charity and powerful intercession, especially at the hour of death. He is also invoked for aid in selling homes or in finding a place to live. In 1870 Pope Pius IX declared him patron of the Universal Church.

Celebrating the Feast Day

Saint Joseph is popular and venerated in many countries around the world. His feast day is celebrated with parades, processions, feasts in the town square, and enactments of the Holy Family's searching for an inn in Bethlehem. In the Latin rite's calendar, his feast day is listed as a holy day of obligation (CIC, canon 1246), although it is not observed as such in the United States or Canada. Many customs have developed from Saint Joseph's role as the protector of the family. He has been invoked in times of famine, and then in gratitude for the end of the famine, he is offered food. Saint Joseph's bread is one such food offering. After being blessed, it is taken home and kept through the year as protection against violent storms and sudden death.

Another custom (that seems to be most popular in North America) is the invocation of Saint Joseph for aid in finding or selling a house. Since Saint Joseph is seen in the Bible searching for lodgings for the Holy Family, he is understood to be especially concerned with homes for families. A statue of Saint Joseph might be displayed prominently near the front of your house, in the living room window for example. (Directions that call for burying the statue in the front or back yard, right side up or upside down, facing the house or facing the street, seem at best disrespectful.) In your daily prayers, ask Saint Joseph's help in finding a new home or a buyer for your home. Remember, in all devotions, it is the intent that displays and develops faith, not the action. The actions or words are important only in that they correctly demonstrate our faith.

Saint Joseph's Bread

Ingredients
- 2¼ cups lukewarm water
- 2 tablespoons active dry yeast
- ¼ cup oil (any kind, though olive oil is suitable)
- 10 cups white flour
- 2 teaspoons salt
- 1 egg yolk mixed with 1 tablespoon water as glaze
- Coarse salt or sesame seeds

Directions

For complete directions in bread making, refer to "Making Bread" in Family Activities.

Sprinkle yeast over water to soften. When it is softened, whisk the oil into the water.

In a large bowl, make a well in the center of the flour and salt. Pour in the yeast mixture. Stir until combined, then knead the dough, first in the bowl, then on a floured counter until it is smooth and stretchy.

Cover and allow to rise until doubled. When your finger leaves an indentation, it has risen sufficiently. Knead again, briefly, then form into loaves. You may put it in bread pans or make free-form loaves or symbolic shapes.

Allow to rise again until almost doubled. Brush the loaves with the egg yolk, and sprinkle with salt or sesame seeds.

Bake at 425°F for 10 minutes, then at 375°F for about 30 minutes more. The bread is done when it is golden brown and the loaves sound hollow when tapped. Cool on a rack.

Prayer

God our Father, You chose Saint Joseph as the husband of Mary, the Mother of Your Son. May he who cared for Your Son here on earth continue to care for us from Your home in heaven, especially as we search for a new home. Through Christ our Lord. Amen.

The Annunciation

Feast day: March 25

The Story of the Annunciation

Sometimes, one action of one person changes life for everyone. We are told in Genesis that Eve and then Adam decided to disobey God and eat "the fruit of the tree of the knowledge of good and evil". That did not seem like much, but it changed all of history. The Annunciation is another very important example.

"Annunciation" sounds like "announcement", and that is just what happened. An angel appeared to Mary and announced that she had found favor with God and would bear a son, Jesus. Saint Luke tells us about it in his Gospel (Lk 1:26–38).

The angel, perhaps in the form of a man, greeted Mary, saying "Hail, full of grace, the Lord is with you!" Mary was confused and did not answer at first. The local tradition of Nazareth states that she fled from him in fear and the angel followed her into the house to continue his message. The angel then told Mary that she had found grace and favor with God, that she was to conceive and bear a son, and that he was to be called Jesus, the Son of the Most High, the Messiah.

Mary was a simple girl from the small town of Nazareth. She was betrothed (engaged) to Joseph, but not yet living with him. When the angel appeared to her, she was frightened and confused. She did not really understand what he was telling her. Why should she be chosen? What did it mean?

"How can [will] this be, since I have no husband?" Mary asked, not out of doubt, like Zechariah, but from astonishment. The angel answered her, saying, "The Holy Spirit will come upon you, and the power of the Most High will overshadow you; therefore the child to be born will be called holy, the Son of God."

This answer could not have reassured or convinced Mary. But, remembering and honoring the angel's earlier words, "the Lord is with you", and trusting God, she answered, "Let it be to me according to your word."

And so, the Incarnation of Jesus began in the simple trusting assent of a humble woman. The Annunciation is the beginning of Jesus' life as a human being. Through His Mother's assent, He is a member of the human race, like us in all things but sin. We are told several times through the Gospel that Mary "treasured all these things in her heart".

Some traditions state that Mary was well educated in the Scriptures and would have known at the moment of her assent that her child would eventually be sacrificed like a lamb for the sins of man. Other traditions hold that Mary understood things only after long pondering and meditation, that she, rather than understanding God's plan, relied on perfect trust and submission to the will of God.

Mary's simple action of saying Yes to God changed everything. Mary became the Mother of God, and our Blessed Mother. Jesus grew up in Nazareth, taught his disciples, and died on the Cross for all our sins. All this happened because Mary said Yes that one time. What a thing to celebrate! What a great reason to love and honor Mary! (See CCC 144, 148.)

The Feast of the Annunciation is celebrated on March 25. It is calculated backward from the date of the Nativity (Christmas).

Though this feast day is named for only one event, the Annunciation, the Church actually commemorates at this time two events important to all mankind. On this day, the Archangel Gabriel appeared to Mary to announce that she was to be the Mother of the Redeemer and Messiah promised for centuries in prophecy. On the same day, the Incarnation took place. God the Son, the second Person of the Trinity, assumed a human body and soul and became the son of Mary and foster son of Joseph.

For most of the Church's history, no feasts were celebrated during Lent. The one exception was this Feast of the Annunciation. The earliest mention of the feast is in the *Sacramentarium* of Pope Gelasius (d. 496). The Toledo and Trullan Synods (656 and 692) refer to the feast as being universally celebrated in the Catholic Church.

Early Christian writers recognized March 25 as the day of the Lord's death as well as of His Incarnation. They argued that the Incarnation of our Lord and His death must have coincided with the creation and fall of Adam, and that since the world was created in spring, the Savior must also have been both conceived and crucified in the spring. Many other events were supposed to have occurred on this day, including the fall of Lucifer, the crossing of the Red Sea, and the offering of Isaac by Abraham.

Celebrating the Feast Day

The Feast of the Annunciation is also known as Lady Day, and girls whose names commemorate Mary may celebrate this as their name day. This would include Maria, Mary, Marie, Madonna, and Mairi. Darica (morning star), Regina (queen), and Abrianna (mother of many nations) could also celebrate this as their name day.

Two symbols are commonly associated with this feast, both symbolizing purity and chastity: the lily and the stork. The lily is well known and used as a symbol for many saints (including Saint Joseph), but today the stork is largely forgotten as an emblem of our Lady. It is associated with the Annunciation because the return of storks to northern towns announced the coming of spring, and in parallel the annunciation to Mary indicated the coming of Christ. The northern European tradition that newborn babies are carried to their mothers by a stork is an extension of this association with the Annunciation.

Remember to add prayers honoring Mary and asking for her protection and intercession to your family prayers. This might be a good time to introduce the much-loved and sometimes forgotten Angelus Prayer to your family. Many hymns sing Mary's praises, among them, "The Angel Gabriel", "Immaculate Mary", "Hail Queen of Heaven, the Ocean Star", and "Salve Regina". They can be found in most hymnals.

The Feast of the Annunciation, like the Feast of the Immaculate Conception, provides a perfect opportunity for some family charitable activity. It is a moment to transform faith and teaching into good works. It could become an annual traditional project for the family.

Mary was engaged but not yet married to Joseph when the angel visited her. She must have been overwhelmed and humbled by what God asked of her. At the same time, while trusting perfectly that God would protect her, she must have also been a little frightened. Her society was not kind to women who became pregnant outside of marriage. She would have been in grave danger if Joseph hadn't heeded the message of the angel in his dream and married her.

To honor Mary's motherhood and to recognize the great gift of every new baby, have the family make a gift to brighten a pregnant mother's day. Some flowers, a potted plant, or a few made-ahead and frozen dinners will really cheer and help a pregnant woman. If you and your family don't know anyone who is expecting a baby, consider giving a similar gift to a pregnancy crisis center.

Your gift doesn't need to be elaborate or expensive to be much appreciated. Homemade stuffed toys, basic toiletries for mom or baby, and simple baby clothes are always needed by these organizations and the mothers they help. As well as honoring and welcoming new life, you will be teaching your family that a gift with love is more splendid than a gift with a big price tag. (See CCC 2447.)

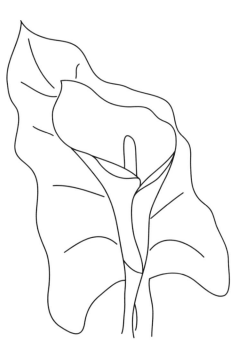

The lily is the flower of the Annunciation. In Renaissance paintings the Angel Gabriel holds a lily, or a lily is placed in a vase between him and the Virgin Mary. Lilies are easily made from a circle of white construction paper wrapped into a cone shape and glued. A yellow strip for a stamen (though in some traditions, the stamens were removed from lilies used at Marian feasts to preserve the purity of the flower) can be glued inside and a smaller green cone and long green strip added as a stem to the bottom. These lilies could be placed around a picture of Mary or could decorate the table.

The Angelus

Verse

The angel of the Lord declared unto Mary.

Response

And she conceived by the Holy Spirit. Hail Mary . . .

Verse

Behold the handmaid of the Lord.

Response

Be it done to me according to your word. Hail Mary . . .

Verse

And the Word was made flesh.

Response

And dwelt among us. Hail Mary . . .

Verse

Pray for us, O holy Mother of God.

Response

That we may be made worthy of the promises of Christ.

Prayer

Pour forth we beseech You, O Lord,
Your grace into our hearts,
that we, to whom the Incarnation of Christ, Your Son,
was made known by the message of an angel,
may by His Passion and Cross
be brought to the glory of His Resurrection.
Through the same Christ our Lord. Amen.

Prayers of or to Mary, Our Mother

The Memorare

Remember, O most gracious Virgin Mary,
that never was it known that anyone
who fled to your protection,
implored your aid,
or sought your intercession
was left unaided.

Inspired by this confidence,
I fly to you,
O Virgin of virgins, my Mother.
To you I come; before you I stand,
sinful and sorrowful;
O Mother of the Word Incarnate,
despise not my petitions,
but in your mercy, hear and answer me.
Amen.

Hail, Holy Queen

Hail, holy Queen, Mother of mercy, our life, our sweetness and
our hope, to you do we cry, poor banished children of Eve, to
you do we send up our sighs, mourning and weeping in this
valley of tears.

Turn then, O most gracious advocate, your eyes of mercy toward
us, and after this our exile, show unto us the blessed fruit of
your womb, Jesus.

O clement, O loving, O sweet Virgin Mary.

V. Pray for us, O holy Mother of God.

R. That we may be made worthy of the promises of Christ.

The Magnificat

"My soul magnifies the Lord,
  and my spirit rejoices in God my Savior,
  for he has regarded the low estate of his handmaiden.
For behold, henceforth all generations will call me blessed;
  for he who is mighty has done great things for me,
  and holy is his name.
And his mercy is on those who fear him
  from generation to generation.
He has shown strength with his arm,
  he has scattered the proud in the imagination of their hearts,
  he has put down the mighty from their thrones,
  and exalted those of low degree;
  he has filled the hungry with good things,
  and the rich he has sent empty away.
He has helped his servant Israel,
  in remembrance of his mercy,
  as he spoke to our fathers,
  to Abraham and to his posterity for ever."

(Lk 1:46–55)

Ave Regina Caelorum

Hail, Queen of Heaven, beyond compare,
to whom the angels homage pay:
Hail, root of Jesse, gate of light,
that opened for the world's new day.

Rejoice, O Virgin unsurpassed,
in whom our ransom was begun,
for all your loving children pray to Christ,
our Savior and your Son.

Saint George

Martyr
Patron of England and of Boy Scouts
Feast day: April 23
Saint George's symbol: dragon

The Life of the Saint

Saint George is known as the dragon slayer. His pictures show him as a brave knight in battle with a fierce dragon. Sometimes there is a beautiful lady in the picture, too. Saint George is fighting the dragon to protect the lady. Dragons represent wickedness and evil and are said to be fierce, cruel, and greedy for treasure and power. Legends say that dragons have fiery breath, long sharp claws, and wings to swoop down on unsuspecting people. They destroy the countryside and scare away all the people. The beautiful lady shown in the pictures represents God's truth and our Holy Mother Church. Saint George is fighting evil to protect the Church!

It would be easy to suppose that Saint George is not a real saint because of the way he is usually depicted: dressed as an English knight of the Middle Ages battling a dragon. Often, Saint George is shown brandishing a sword with the dragon's body wrapped around him like a giant constrictor. A castle in the background, complete with a fair maiden wringing her hands on a parapet, finishes off the picture.

But this is all symbolic. Saint George was a real man, a soldier in the early fourth century at the beginning of the Diocletian persecution of Christians. Some accounts say that he was one of the emperor Diocletian's favorites. Other stories say that when Diocletian caused a proclamation against Christians to be printed and posted in Nicomedia, it was George who tore it down, denounced the new law, and publicly proclaimed his faith.

It is certainly known that George was arrested, tried, tortured, and finally executed as a Christian. It is also known that he resisted the demands of the torturers that he deny his faith and worship the Roman gods. Very soon after his martyrdom, many legends sprang up around the true story of George, claiming that he returned to life three times and that wonderful cures and other miracles surrounded him.

Devotion to this saint extends back to the fifth century. If it can be proved that one of the oldest churches in Constantinople dedicated to his name was actually built by Constantine the Great, then devotion to Saint George is even older than that.

Saint George was known and revered in England by the eighth century. A church in Doncaster, England, dedicated to Saint George was built in 1006. His popularity grew under the influence of the Crusades. He is said to have been seen fighting along with the Franks at the battle of Antioch. It is probable that the arms of Saint George were introduced at about the time of Richard Coeur de Lion, perhaps to reinforce the morale and conviction of the Crusaders. The large red Saint George's cross on a white ground is one of the elements in the British flag (called the Union Jack) today, and he is the patron saint of England.

Regardless of how much of his story is true, this much is certain. As a soldier, Saint George understood better than many of the early Christian martyrs just what would happen to him when he proclaimed his faith. He approached this as he must have approached many battles: brave, scared, but determined to acquit himself with honor. We can learn from his example when we face trials, battles, and challenges in our lives today.

We are all called to be soldiers for Christ. Legend or not, dragons or other forms of evil, fair maidens or the purity and truth of the Church, Saint George shows us the way to defend our faith. All soldiers need to know strategy and fighting skills; Saint George was among them. His faith and knowledge will be at our aid if we ask for it, and he will intercede for us to God for help in all our battles.

> Proclaiming Your glory, Lord,
> we humbly ask
> that as Saint George imitated Christ in His Passion
> so he may be a ready helper in our weakness.
> We make our prayer through our Lord,
> who lives and reigns forever. Amen.

Celebrating the Feast Day

During the time of Moorish (Muslim) invasions of Spain (which lasted nearly seven hundred years) the Spanish people recognized Saint George as an ally in their struggle to protect the Catholic Church and their country. He is still revered in that country today and honored at festivals celebrating the defeat of the Moors.

Remember to add prayers asking for the aid and intercession of Saint George to your family prayers. Ask each person to tell of a particular battle in his life (resisting a schoolyard bully or persisting in witnessing in the workplace, for example) and ask for Saint George's guidance in these situations.

Read the life of the saint out loud, either from this book or from the many other excellent lives of the saints available in bookstores, libraries, or on-line. Point out that the dragon is a very old, very enduring symbol of danger and evil. Read chapters 6 and 7, "The Adventures of Eustace" and "How the Adventures Ended", in *The Voyage of the Dawn Treader* from C. S. Lewis' Narnia series, and talk about the dragon in that story.

A popular Spanish and Cuban dish, appropriate both to the Feast of Saint George and Lent, is black beans and rice.

Black Beans and Rice

Ingredients
- 2 cups black turtle beans
- 5 slices bacon, chopped (optional)
- 1 onion, chopped
- 1 clove garlic, or more, chopped
- 1 teaspoon dry basil
- 1 bay leaf (optional)
- 1 teaspoon cumin
- 1 teaspoon (or more) red pepper flakes
- Salt to taste
- Lemon juice and lemon wedges
- White rice, cooked

Directions

Soak beans overnight (or use quick-soak method: cover beans with water, bring to a boil, then let stand for an hour). Drain.

Partially cook bacon in a large pot (omit if the feast falls on a Friday); add drained beans, onion, and garlic and all seasonings except salt. Cover with water. Bring to a boil, and allow to simmer until beans are tender. This will take about an hour.

The beans should be juicy, but not soupy. If there is too much liquid still, pour some off. Add salt and lemon juice to taste.

Serve over cooked rice. Garnish with a lemon wedge and some chopped tomatoes.

He who believes and is baptized will be saved, but he who does not believe will be condemned. And these signs will

accompany those who believe: in my name they will cast out demons; they will speak in new tongues; they will pick up

Prayer

Lord, we acclaim Your might and humbly pray. Just as Saint George imitated the Lord's Passion, so let him now come to the aid of our weakness. Amen.

Our Father

Our Father Who art in Heaven,
   hallowed be Thy name.
Thy kingdom come,
Thy will be done on earth as it is in Heaven.
Give us this day our daily bread,
   and forgive us our trespasses as we forgive those who trespass
   against us.
And lead us not into temptation, but deliver us from evil. Amen.

Hail Mary

Hail, Mary, full of grace, the Lord is with thee.
Blessed art thou amongst women,
   and blessed is the fruit of thy womb, Jesus.
Holy Mary, Mother of God, pray for us sinners,
   now and at the hour of our death. Amen.

Apostles' Creed

I believe in God, the Father almighty,
   Creator of heaven and earth.
I believe in Jesus Christ, his only Son, our Lord.
He was conceived by the power of the Holy Spirit
   and born of the Virgin Mary.
He suffered under Pontius Pilate,
   was crucified, died and was buried.

He descended into hell.
On the third day he rose again.
He ascended into heaven
   and is seated at the right hand of the Father.
He will come again to judge the living and the dead.
I believe in the Holy Spirit,
   the holy catholic Church,
   the communion of saints,
   the forgiveness of sins,
   the resurrection of the body,
   and the life everlasting. Amen.

A Hymn for Saint George

Leader now on earth no longer,
Soldier of th'eternal King,
Victor in the fight for heaven,
We thy loving praises sing.

   Great Saint George, our patron, help us,
   In the conflict be thou nigh;
   Help us in that daily battle,
   Where each one must win or die.

Praise him who in deadly battle
Never shrank from foeman's sword,
Proof against all earthly weapon,
Gave his life for Christ the Lord.

   Great Saint George, etc.

Who, when earthly war was over,
Fought, but not for earth's renown;
Fought, and won a nobler glory,
Won the martyr's purple crown.

   Great Saint George, etc.

Crafts

that Jesus began to do and teach, until the day when he was taken up, after he had given commandment through the

Making Easter Eggs

Unlike the Easter bunny with which they are so often associated, Easter eggs have a legitimate place in Easter observances and in Lenten preparations.

Enclosing and protecting the little chicks, eggs represent new life in the world, and so they also represent new life in the Church. With their smooth, hard shell hiding the life within, they symbolize hidden promise, Christ coming out of the tomb.

Decorating eggs for Easter, placing symbols of Christ and the Resurrection on their surface, is an obvious and natural extension of this significance. The Ukrainian culture is well known for its decorated eggs called *pysanky*, though other traditions decorate eggs as well. Traditional symbols for Easter eggs and *pysanky* include:

• Wheat: the bread of Life
• Fish: symbol of Christ
• Birds: an ancient image of the soul
• Triangles: the Trinity
• Spots: the tears of Mary
• Red: the blood of Christ
• Stars, roses, and poppies: love, charity, and good will
• Cross-hatching: both the crown of thorns and the tools that Christ used during his hidden years

There are several beautiful Ukrainian legends linking Easter eggs and the Blessed Virgin Mary. One tells that Mary filled her apron with eggs. When she appeared before Pontius Pilate to plead for her Son, she dropped to her knees, and the eggs rolled out over the world until they were distributed to all the nations. (There is an interesting parallel between this legend, which is certainly several hundred years old, and the image of Mary on Juan Diego's cloak half a world away in Mexico.) Another legend describes the traditional dots on the eggs as representing the tears of the Virgin, who gave eggs to the soldiers at the Cross. As she begged them to be less cruel, she wept, and her tears fell on the eggs, giving them brilliant dots of color.

Many families set aside a day or two for decorating Easter eggs (Good Friday and Holy Saturday in the midst of the spring cleaning is one choice), while others work on more elaborate eggs all through Lent. Some families we know set up a card table in a quiet corner and keep all their supplies there. Any time someone has a spare moment, he can just sit down and work on his egg. There are a wide variety of methods for decorating eggs (and other egglike shapes), some requiring a high level of skill, others needing only enthusiasm. For example:

Papier-Mâché Eggs

These are good for younger children to make and decorate, because they are larger and therefore easier for small hands to handle. They are also less likely to break than an egg. Papier-mâché eggs can also be filled piñata-style with candies and small devotional objects and used for Easter morning. Children can manage all but the last step of preparing these eggs. You will only need to supervise according to age.

Materials

- Regular size balloons
- Newspaper
- White glue or wallpaper paste
- Poster paint or markers
- Varnish (spray varnish in a can would be most convenient)

Making the Papier-Mâché Egg

Blow up a regular-size balloon to about a six-inch egg shape and knot it securely.

Tear newspaper into strips. Do not cut it, tear it. The ragged edges of torn strips mesh together better and make stronger, smoother papier-mâché.

Next, make a mix of watered-down glue or wallpaper paste for adhesive.

Saturate one torn strip of newsprint in the glue. Apply it to the small balloon. Cover the balloon one strip at a time. Do not apply the strips on top of the knot of the balloon (where it has been tied). Work around this opening, maintaining the smooth shape of the egg. When the egg is completely covered with four or five layers of paper (but if the kids are having fun, more will not hurt), set it aside to dry overnight.

The next morning, pierce the balloon and remove the tattered remains. (Dispose of these where little ones will not chew on them and choke.) Allow the egg to dry just a little more, and then apply an additional layer of papier-mâché. If you want to fill your eggs, do so now, then cover the balloon knothole with papier-mâché. Allow the egg to dry thoroughly.

Finally, decorate the eggs with paint or markers. Crayons or colored pencils probably will not work as well, because the surface is too bumpy. Simple stripes or dots look great; so do zigzags and pictures. Paint a coat of varnish on the egg for a shiny finish. (An adult should take care of this last step.)

Decorated Real Eggs

Eggs can be blown, dyed fresh (unblown), or hard-boiled. Blown eggs are more fragile, and blowing them without having a large unsightly hole is tricky. Fresh, unblown eggs can be used (they will gradually dry out), but they make a real mess if they break while you are dying them, and they really stink if they break three weeks later. Hard-boiled eggs will not last at all, but they are the most durable for family use; you will just be eating egg salad for a week or so after Easter.

Natural Dyes

A number of colors are possible from simple ingredients you can find in your kitchen, in case you forgot to buy coloring or do not want to use food coloring or those funny tablet things. These colors will be paler than the artificial dyes, and it takes a bit more time to create designs on eggs using natural dyes, but it is still possible. The general method for preparing and using natural dyes is as follows:

Put your eggs in a single layer in a pan. Pour water in the pan until the eggs are covered, and add about a teaspoon of vinegar.

Next add the natural dye material for the color you want your eggs to be. (The more eggs you are dying at a time, the more dye you will need to use.) Bring water to a boil, then reduce heat and simmer for fifteen minutes. Obviously, this method will produce very hard-boiled eggs. Remove the eggs from the pot, and put them in a bowl to cool and dry. If you want your eggs to be a darker shade, cover them with the dye and let them stand overnight in the refrigerator.

The colors possible with natural dyes are:

- **Pale red:** fresh beets or cranberries, frozen raspberries
- **Orange:** yellow onion skins
- **Light yellow:** orange or lemon peels, carrot tops, celery seed, or ground cumin
- **Yellow:** ground turmeric
- **Pale green:** spinach leaves
- **Green-gold:** Yellow Delicious apple peels
- **Blue:** canned blueberries or red cabbage leaves
- **Beige to brown:** strong brewed coffee

Food-Coloring Dyes

This is one of the easier and cheaper ways to dye Easter eggs. The dyes found in Easter egg-dying kits sold in grocery stores are not really any better. Besides, if you do not buy the kits, you do not have to explain why the Easter bunny or a cartoon character is not really suitable for decorating an Easter egg. Your children's creativity gets to develop without commercial influences.

To make a food-coloring dye: In a fairly deep cup, such as a coffee cup or a small bowl, mix about twenty drops of food coloring with one teaspoon of vinegar. Add one-half cup hot water, then let the water cool to room temperature. You want the coloring to cover the egg completely when put in the cup, so mix up more dye if necessary. Repeat the steps above to make as many different colors as you want, mixing dyes to make colors such as purple or orange.

Gently lower eggs into the cup. This is easiest with a piece of wire with a loop on one end bent at a right angle to the rest of the wire. The longer you leave the eggs in the dye, the darker the colors will be. Once the egg reaches the desired color, remove it from the cup with your wire loop, and let dry on a wire rack (the kind you cool cakes and cookies on).

Adding Designs to Your Eggs

Simple single-color eggs are certainly faster than decorated eggs. They look nice piled in a bowl as a centerpiece. If single-color eggs are all you have time or skill for, stick with that. If you want to try something more elaborate, here are a few ideas, starting with the simplest.

Dipped Eggs   Dye eggs a light color, such as yellow or pink. This will be your background color. Allow to dry. Hold the egg carefully in the egg holder and lower it halfway into another dye container. (You can bend the handle of your egg holder over the edge of the cup at the desired depth if you wish.)

Hold it there as long as you want, then remove the egg and allow it to dry. The longer you hold it in the dye, the more intense the color.

Tie-Dye Eggs   Dye eggs a light color, such as yellow or pink, as your background color. Allow to dry. Wrap one or two elastic bands around the egg in a random pattern. Dye the egg with a darker color. Allow to dry, and remove the elastic bands. If you want, repeat the process with a third color.

Masking-Tape Eggs   Dye eggs a background color, such as yellow or pink. Allow to dry. Stick thin strips of masking tape on the egg, around the long and short circumference, dividing it into sections. Dye the egg with a darker color. Allow to dry and remove the masking tape. If you want, leave the first tape in place, put more masking tape in the spaces, and dye with a third color. Allow the egg to dry, then remove the masking tape.

Scratched or Resist Eggs   This method allows slightly more elaborate patterns with finer lines. This is not a good method to use with young children, because it uses melted paraffin wax and hot water. Always melt wax slowly over water in a double boiler or in a soup can placed in a pot of water. You need enough wax in a container to cover the egg completely. As soon as it is all melted, remove it from the heat.

Dye eggs a light color, such as yellow or pink. This will be your background color. Allow to dry. After the egg is dry, dip it into melted paraffin wax. After the wax is dry, etch your design by scratching through the wax with a darning needle. Make sure you scratch all the wax off your design. Then dip the egg into another color of dye. Because of the wax coating, only the lines you scratched will pick up the new color.

If you want, scratch more designs on the egg and dye it in a third color, or re-wax your egg to preserve the second color pattern and scratch more patterns. Dye the egg again and allow to dry. Remove the wax by heating the egg slightly in hot water, and polish the surface by rubbing in any remaining wax.

Pysanky (Decorated Ukrainian Eggs)

The procedure for making *pysanky* is the same for each egg. The designs vary from egg to egg. Making *pysanky* is not difficult, but it does take a lot of practice and a special tool called a *kistka*.

The *kistka*, a hollow brass cone with a pinhole that is attached to a wooden rod, is the tool used to draw with hot beeswax onto a raw (uncooked) or blown egg. The *kistka*, Ukrainian for "little bone", has progressed from a small bone strapped to a stick to a copper or brass cone. The wax in the tool is heated either by the flame of a candle or by electricity. You may be able to create a *kistka*-type tool yourself, with a pencil, wire, and a small cone of metal. A second-best alternative I have used is a toothpick to paint the melted wax onto the egg. Results are best with a real *kistka*.

Kistkas and *pysanky* dyes, which come in a wide range of colors from yellow to black, are available at Ukrainian supply shops, often in shops at Ukrainian churches, and are also available on-line at: http://www.yevshan.com/main.asp/.

It is also important to try to get beeswax, which sticks to the egg better and prevents the dye from seeping under the edges onto areas where you do not want it. Between steps, you may leave the egg resting on a cake rack or on toothpicks stuck into thick cardboard. *Pysanky* can take several days to make.

Making Pysanky

Step One Starting with a raw (uncooked) or blown egg, lightly sketch with pencil the main division lines on the egg. All the patterns are drawn freehand on the egg.

Then, heat the *kistka*, melting the beeswax, so that it flows freely and forms thin lines of wax. All lines that you want to remain white are drawn first on the egg with melted beeswax. The wax acts like a protective covering, keeping the areas you have covered white when you put it into the first dye bath. Successive additions of wax and dyes will create your patterns.

Step One

Once all the lines that are to be white are covered with wax, dip the entire egg into the yellow dye bath. Any part of the eggshell that is not covered with wax will turn yellow.

Step Two Next, all parts of the pattern that you want to remain yellow get covered with wax to seal in the yellow color.

Step Two

When you have covered all the yellow spaces in the pattern, dip the egg into the orange dye bath. The wax covering the white and yellow parts of the design is still on the egg. The wax needs to stay in place until all the designing of the egg is done.

Step Three As before, all parts of the design that are to remain orange now get covered and protected with wax while the egg is orange. When this is complete, dip the egg in the red dye bath. Be careful not to rub or knock any of the wax covering off.

Step Three

Step Four   The red color on the egg should be the most predominant color in a *pysanka*. All aspects of the design to carry the red color are covered with wax. This will probably be most of the remaining space on your egg. Then the egg is dipped into the last and darkest dye bath, black.

Some Traditional Pysanky Outlines and Images

Step Five   Once the egg is removed from the black dye bath, it will look like this. Now, the exciting part begins.

All the wax that was applied from the very beginning can now be removed. By holding the egg next to a candle flame, slowly melt the wax off. Be careful not to hold the egg over the flame; it will become blackened with candle soot.

Step Five

Step Four

You may gently heat the eggs in the oven on a rack made of nails driven halfway into a board. Watch them closely so that they do not get too hot.

Rub the egg gently with a soft absorbent cloth to remove the wax, frequently switching to a new spot on the rag. Old t-shirts and flannelette pajamas work well here, not paper towels, which can leave fibers stuck in the wax.

Step Six   The vibrant colors of the completed egg shine through. Apply a coat of high-gloss varnish (your fingers work best for this job) for preservation and the finishing touch. Your *pysanky* will last for generations. (If children under fourteen have made the *pysanky*, an adult should take care of the final step of varnishing them.)

Step Six

Lent and Easter in the Domestic Church: Crafts   www.Domestic-Church.com

Alms Boxes

Some families collect money all through Lent to bring as their Lenten offering to Easter Mass. (See CCC 1434.) They collect these alms from the money they would have spent on candy, dessert, or cigarettes, choosing to give it to the poor instead.

A special alms box can make collecting alms throughout Lent more interesting for the family. It can be made in a wide variety of ways. Your family alms box, once completed, can be placed on the family altar, in the center of the family table during meals, or in some other prominent place where it will be easy to put coins into it every day.

Papier-Mâché Alms Box Follow the papier-mâché directions from page 59, covering a balloon blown to its biggest with at least four layers of papier-mâché. When you remove the balloon and cover the knot hole with more papier-mâché, cut a slit on the opposite side wide enough and long enough for a coin or a folded bill.

Cover the alms box with a few more layers of papier-mâché, then allow it to dry well. Decorate with paint, markers, torn scraps of tissue paper, or whatever else you like. Consider adding the words "We share with our neighbors" or some other expression of charity to the box.

You might want to make an alms box for every member of the family, or you may prefer to make one large one, showing that your community of love (your family) acts together to take care of others.

Mosaic Alms Box Find a suitably sized cardboard box: a square tissue box, a small cereal box, or a table salt box. Tape thin cardboard over the dispenser opening of the tissue box; tape the end of the cereal box closed; or pry the pour-spout off the salt box.

Cut a slit wide enough and long enough for a coin or a folded bill on the top or side of your prepared container. Glue pasta shapes, small shells, colored sand, or small eggshell pieces into

patterns on the top and sides of the box, and allow the glue to dry well. If you want, you can shake the pasta shapes, sand, or eggshells in (water-soluble) poster paint or food coloring before you glue them onto your box.

Otherwise, you can paint the box and its glued-on decorations as you wish or spray-paint your box with gold spray paint. Set aside and allow to dry well before using.

Tin Can Alms Box A one-pound coffee can with a reusable plastic lid makes a sturdy alms box.

Cut a strip of paper the height of the can, and wrap the paper around the can to figure out how long to cut it. Be sure to allow enough overlap to be able to fasten it securely. Remove the paper.

Let the children decorate the paper with scenes of poverty, of almsgiving, or other acts of charity, a prayer, or whatever comes from their imagination and understanding of almsgiving. You can discuss ideas with them first, to explore and expand their knowledge of this devotional practice. Decorations can be made with paint, crayons, markers, stickers, or colored pencils. If no one is feeling inspired, you can cut out pictures and letters from a magazine or parish bulletin about Lenten offerings and glue them in place.

When the paper is ready, tape it around the can and replace the plastic lid.

Preparing Your Alms

Counting and rolling coins is great counting and calculating practice for children. Making the little piles of coins, then rolling them in the papers is also good dexterity practice.

Ask for coin-rolling papers at your local bank. Most banks will be happy to give them to you for free, along with any special instructions for exchanging them. Your parish office will thank you for saving them this work!

Making Banners

Banners are an increasingly popular form of decoration. The nice thing, of course, is that banners are teaching tools as well as decoration. With words and images they convey a message.

Seen as teaching tools rather than simply as a modern craft, banners have great evangelizing and catechetical potential in the home, as well as in the classroom and parish. They can be hung in any room or hallway to proclaim your faith to all who view them.

Banners are very flexible. They can be any size or color, any style or image. They can be simple or ornate depending on your time, budget, and ability. They can be made of almost anything and used for almost any occasion. In fact, they are so simple, yet potentially so powerful, that every family should consider making several to fit various family and liturgical celebrations.

Banners can be made of any firm cloth or backed with a sturdy cloth to help them hang flat and straight. Felt, burlap, and canvas are obvious choices, but moiré fabric or lightweight broadcloth are other good choices. Banners for use outside work well in broadcloth, canvas, or nylon. Depending on the style of the banner and your abilities, decorations can be drawn on with waterproof markers, fabric paint, or acrylic paint, or glued or sewn on. Images and letters can be made of buttons, ribbon, braid, strings of wool, or anything else you might have. Since the variety is almost endless, I will outline a few of the possibilities and leave the rest up to you and your family's imagination!

A Saint's Day Banner

A saint's day banner (once it is made) is a fast and easy special decoration reserved for this family event. The banner can be hung as part of a triduum (three-day) preparation for the feast day or hung on the actual feast day. Any symbol of sainthood or heaven can be used on the banner, such as flames, doves, or crowns. There are many other possibilities. The symbols

for each individual name saint could be added to the banner for a family portrait of saints' symbols, or interchangeable symbols fastened with Velcro dots or a snap fastener could personalize the banner for each feast.

A Lent and Easter Banner

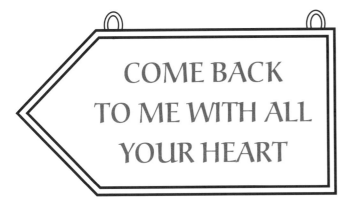

COME BACK
TO ME WITH ALL
YOUR HEART

This reversible banner is our main Lenten decoration. On Ash Wednesday I put away all our other pictures, statues, icons, and knickknacks except crucifixes and hang this banner. On Holy Saturday, I bring out all our Easter decorations and flip the banner.

Special decorations reserved for special occasions strengthen the importance of the celebration and help create the traditions necessary to pass the faith down successive generations.

I found the phrase "Come Back to Me with All Your Heart" (Joel 2:12) at the back of a missal and used it because I liked the personal tone. You may find that some other phrase appeals to you, has more significance, or conveys a clearer Lenten message to you and your family.

Rejoice!

In the same way, the Easter side of the banner can say whatever seems most appropriate to you. It would be best if the colors chosen were liturgically appropriate.

Festive Party Banners

Special banners just for special celebrations like birthday or graduation parties are worth the effort for the message of love and respect they give the recipient of the celebration: "Your party gets the special decorations."

Windsock banners take a little more time but are surprisingly easy to make and store. They look great blowing in the wind and can be hung from trees, hooks, your clothesline, or poles stuck in the ground.

Cut strips of brightly colored fabric as long as you would like the finished windsock to be. If you are going to use eight strips, make each one one-eighth of your desired finished diameter plus an inch (for a half-inch seam allowance on each side).

Mark a spot halfway down the length of each strip, and sew the strips together from the top to the marked spot. The rest will hang free and blow in the wind. Do not sew the last two strips together to complete the circle yet, though. Hem the loose ends of each strip. It does not have to be perfect, just turn under the edge and sew it. Go down one long side, along the bottom edge, up the other long side, then, without cutting the thread, repeat with the next strip. Now sew the last strips together to form a circle.

called in their language Akeldama, that is, Field of Blood.) For it is written in the book of Psalms, 'Let his habitation become desolate, and let there be no one to live in it'; and

middle and all his bowels gushed out. And it became known to all the inhabitants of Jerusalem, so that the field was

Turn under the circular top edge about one-half inch, and sew it, leaving an inch-long opening between your starting and finishing place.

Find something fairly firm, such as a wire coat hanger or plastic tubing, and feed it into the channel you have just sewn at the top of your banner. This will hold the mouth of the windsock in a circle.

Next, attach three strings at equal distance around the rim of the windsock. Tie the strings together at the top and make a loop for hanging.

I made a dozen of these windsock banners one evening as part of the decorations for a wedding reception held in our backyard and have used them several times since. When not in use, they are stored on a hanger in a closet with the winter coats.

Some Useful Stitches

Satin Stitch Make straight, evenly spaced stitches to fill in an area. If you want, you can outline the area with running stitch or some other stitch first.

Couching Lay a thread or yarn along the line of the design (like a letter or shape) and with another thread fasten it down along its length. This is a fast and easy way to form letters.

Buttonhole Stitch This stitch can be used to sew another piece of fabric onto your banner, such as a flame or a crown. It has a decorative effect, especially if the stitches are even in size and spacing.

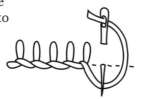

SOME SAMPLE ALPHABETS

abcdefghijklmnopqrstuvwxyz
ABCDEFGHIJKLMNO
PQRSTUVWXYZ

abcdefghijklmnopqrstuvwxyz
ABCDEFGHIJKLMNO
PQRSTUVWXYZ

abcdefghijklmnopqrstuvwxyz
ABCDEFGHIJKLMNO
PQRSTUVWXYZ

abcdefghijklmnopqrstuvwxyz
ABCDEFGHIJKLMNO
PQRSTUVWXYZ

abcdefghijklmnopqrstuvwxyz
ABCDEFGHIJKLMNO
PQRSTUVWXYZ

Holy Water for Your Home

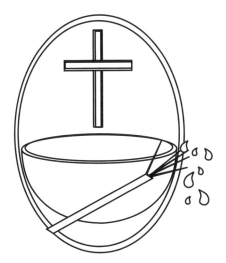

Every home should have a font for holy water by the front door, so that the family members can bless themselves as they enter and leave the house. This echoes both the blessing of the water at the Easter vigil and the Epiphany (CCC 1238, 1668–70).

Holy water can also be used at evening prayers to bless the children before they head off to bed. The father, in his office as head of the family (as Christ is Head of the Church), should bless his children every day.

These special moments express his love and caring protection of them and give them the graces and confidence necessary to face both the challenges and trials of their growing lives. Holy water is also useful to bless a new house, a new car, the bedroom of the latest child having nightmares, an Advent wreath, the Christmas tree, and the Easter feast, and it may be used for other family celebrations and devotions.

Blessed holy water should be available at your church after Easter. Some churches have special dispensers with taps for holy water at the back of the church. In other parishes, you may have to ask the priest or sacristan for holy water. Bring a small bottle with you.

A useful little item is a "holy water sprinkler". Any member of the family old enough to handle a pocket knife can make one. The most important thing to remember when using a knife is to cut away from yourself.

Never point or push the knife blade toward your hand or body!

All you need is a six-inch stick from a tree or bush and your pocket knife.

- Carefully peel the bark off the stick.
- Carve one end of the stick to a neat blunt point, just so that it is not raggedy.
- Split the other end of the stick in half by standing the stick up on a surface and gently pushing the knife blade down-

ward into it. Keep both hands on the back of the blade and use the pressure of the knife to keep the stick upright.

- Alternatively, you can lay the stick down on a cutting board or piece of wood outside (not on Mom's counter or dining room table!) and slice into the end of the stick. If you are right-handed, hold the stick in your left hand with the end you want to cut pointing to the right. If you are left-handed, hold the stick with your right hand with the end you want to cut pointing to the left.
- Split about half an inch into the stick. Split it again into quarters, then eighths, then sixteenths, until the end of the stick is like frayed rope.

And it's done!

Make several and give them away to your friends and relatives. Keep one with each font and bottle of holy water (recycled, small spice bottles are perfect for holy water). The holy water sprinkler is used by dipping it into the holy water and flicking the drops off its end, just as the priest does at Mass.

Shrines and Stations

Children love collecting stuff. Little boys collect rocks and sticks and small metal cars, bent nails, pieces of paper, and the occasional insect. Little girls collect doll parts, costume jewelry, pretty rocks (these are sometimes indistinguishable from little boy rocks), plastic hair barrettes, and coloring pictures.

If given the opportunity, girls and boys love collecting cards too. And if given the opportunity, they will collect holy cards, Mass cards, and saints' cards as avidly as any other type. Since these kinds of cards and portraits foster their spiritual development and give healthy imagery to their imaginations, why not encourage collecting them?

One way to encourage enjoyment and appreciation of holy cards is to provide craft ideas using holy cards. Some families put them into photo albums with stories of the lives of the saints and prayers. Others buy or make simple frames to hang the holy cards in the children's rooms. Here's another craft idea: making small shrines.

Depending on the image on the cards these shrines can be used for Stations of the Cross, small shrines for a name saint, in a prayer corner, or at the family altar. For the family Stations of the Cross, use the images found in the following "Coloring Pictures" section. Pictures drawn by child or parent could replace holy cards if the subject you want is not available.

Popsicle-Stick Shrines

Materials

- White glue
- Popsicle sticks or tongue depressors
- Plasticine or play dough
- A selection of pictures
- Craft paint, markers, beads, medals, and other decorative things (optional)

Directions

Working on a flat surface, lay two Popsicle sticks at an angle to each other, with the tips just touching. These are the beginning pieces of the roof.

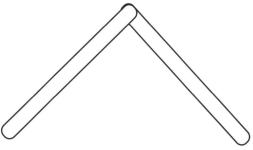

Arrange them so that the roof slope is neither too wide nor too steep to fit your holy card. Test this by laying two Popsicle sticks in place as side walls. Check that your shrine will be tall enough to fit the picture.

When you are satisfied with the arrangement, glue the two roof pieces together. Allow the glue to dry. Brace it with pieces of plasticine, if necessary, to keep the roof pieces at the correct angle. You can also use a clothespin as a clamp to hold the pieces while the glue dries.

Next, glue two side wall pieces onto the roof pieces, laying and gluing a floor piece under the two side wall pieces at the same time, as shown in the first illustration on page 69. Allow the glue to dry.

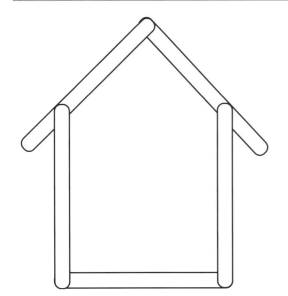

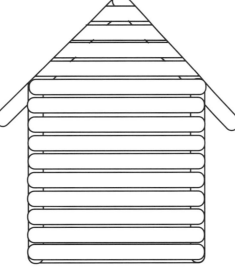

Make another layer of two roof pieces, two side wall pieces, and a floor piece. This time glue all five pieces at the same time. Allow the glue to dry. Repeat this layering another three or four times, depending on how deep you want your shrine or station to be.

When the shrine is deep enough, glue on a back wall, with Popsicle sticks laid horizontally across the back (*illustration above right*). You will have to trim the pieces in the peak of the roof. (Children above the age of eight can safely use a small hacksaw, or an adult can cut the pieces with a sharp kitchen knife.)

Turn the shrine over, front face up. Using four small segments of Popsicle sticks, add another two layers of floor, so that the floor extends a bit to the front, as shown in the illustration at right.

Glue your picture, holy card, or station into the shrine, and set it aside to dry.

Catholic gift shops, religious goods stores, and your parish priest are possible sources of holy cards. There are also mail order companies supplying holy cards and other devotionals to families. Try a web search for them, or, if you know the company name, call 1-800-555-1212 for their toll-free number.

Guardian Angel Cross-Stitch

God created the angels to praise Him in heaven and to guide and protect us. Some of these angels are the guardian angels. They guard us against evil and, as God's messengers, help us know what God wants us to do. (See CCC 328–30.)

Every person in the world has an angel whose only job is to watch over him, pray for him to God, and keep him safe from sin and evil. If you listen well, your angel will keep your soul from sin and protect your body from harm. Have you ever almost fallen down, or nearly been hurt some other way, and had someone say, "Your guardian angel is watching over you"?

Our guardian angel loves us because God loves us. He loves us because we are so precious to God that His only Son Jesus died on the Cross to save us. Our angel wants us to go to heaven, to live with God forever. We can ask our guardian angel for help by saying the prayer; it will remind us to keep listening for the guidance of our own special angel (CCC 336).

I created this simple cross-stitch sampler for my children to work. It helped them learn the prayer and made a beautiful addition to their bedrooms.

This piece is 242 squares wide and 82 squares high. On 12-count Aida cloth, the finished piece will measure 20 inches by 7 inches. On 16-count Aida cloth, the finished pieces will measure 15 inches by 5¼ inches. I find that finer, 18-count Aida cloth is too hard on the eyes. Some extra cloth on all sides will be needed to frame the prayer, so purchase cloth a few inches larger all around than the dimensions quoted here.

The angel outlines and most of the letters are done in running stitch using two strands of embroidery cotton. Cross-stitch using three strands of cotton fills the outlines of the angel and forms the words Angel and God. (I have made a few color combination suggestions in the chart key, but choose colors that you like, that you have, or that suit your decor.)

How to Cross-Stitch

Bring the thread through at the lower right-hand side, insert the needle 1 block up and 1 block to the left and bring out 1 block down, thus forming a half cross; continue in this way to the end of the row. Complete the upper half of the cross as shown.

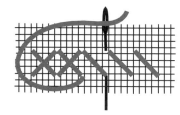

Cross-stitch may be worked either from right to left or left to right, but it is important that the upper stroke of all crosses lie in the same direction.

How to Do Running Stitch

Running stitch and backstitch are the same basic stitch; the difference lies in which side of the fabric you are looking at. Backstitch looks thicker and fuller than running stitch.

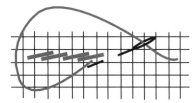

Both are a "two steps forward and one step back" kind of stitch. After coming through the fabric, run the needle across two blocks, then down. Bring the needle back one block, and bring it up through the fabric again. Run it two blocks, then down, and so on.

Colors Used for All Color Variations

Cream—DMC 712 (Wings)
Tan—ultra very light DMC 739 (Wing edge)
Flesh—medium DMC 945 (Face and hands)
Coffee Brown—dark DMC 801 (Eyes)
Coffee Brown—dark DMC 801 (Outlining)

For Blue Angels

Straw—light DMC 3822 (Hair and cross-stitch letters)
Royal Blue—DMC 797 (Body and far arm of coat)
Royal Blue—dark DMC 796 (Near arm of coat)
Delft—dark DMC 798 (Gown)
Christmas Red—dark DMC 498 (Contrast edging and shoes)
Royal Blue—dark DMC 796 (Running stitch letters)

For Red Angels

Coffee Brown—very dark DMC 898 (Hair and cross-stitch letters)
Garnet—medium DMC 815 (Body and far arm of coat)
Garnet—dark DMC 814 (Near arm of coat)
Garnet—very dark DMC 902 (Gown)
Ecru—(Contrast edging and shoes)
Garnet—very dark DMC 902 (Running stitch letters)

For Green Angels

Golden Brown—medium DMC 976 (Hair and cross-stitch letters)
Christmas Green—bright DMC 700 (Body and far arm of coat)
Christmas Green—DMC 699 (Near arm of coat)
Forest Green—DMC 989 (Gown)
Old Gold—very light DMC 677 (Contrast edging and shoes)
Christmas Green—DMC 699 (Running stitch letters)

For Purple Angels

Mahogany—very dark DMC 300 (Hair and cross-stitch letters)
Grape—medium DMC 3835 (Body and far arm of coat)
Grape—dark DMC 3834 (Near arm of coat)
Grape—light DMC 3836 (Gown)
Old Gold—light DMC 676 (Contrast edging and shoes)
Violet—very dark DMC 550 (Running stitch letters)

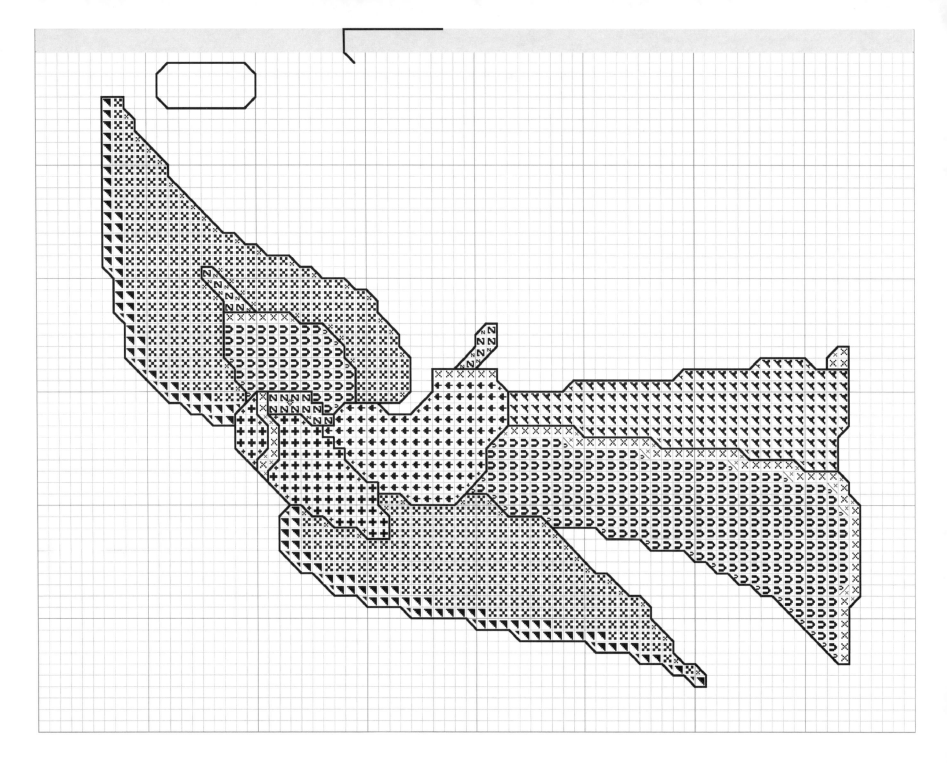

Lent and Easter in the Domestic Church: Crafts

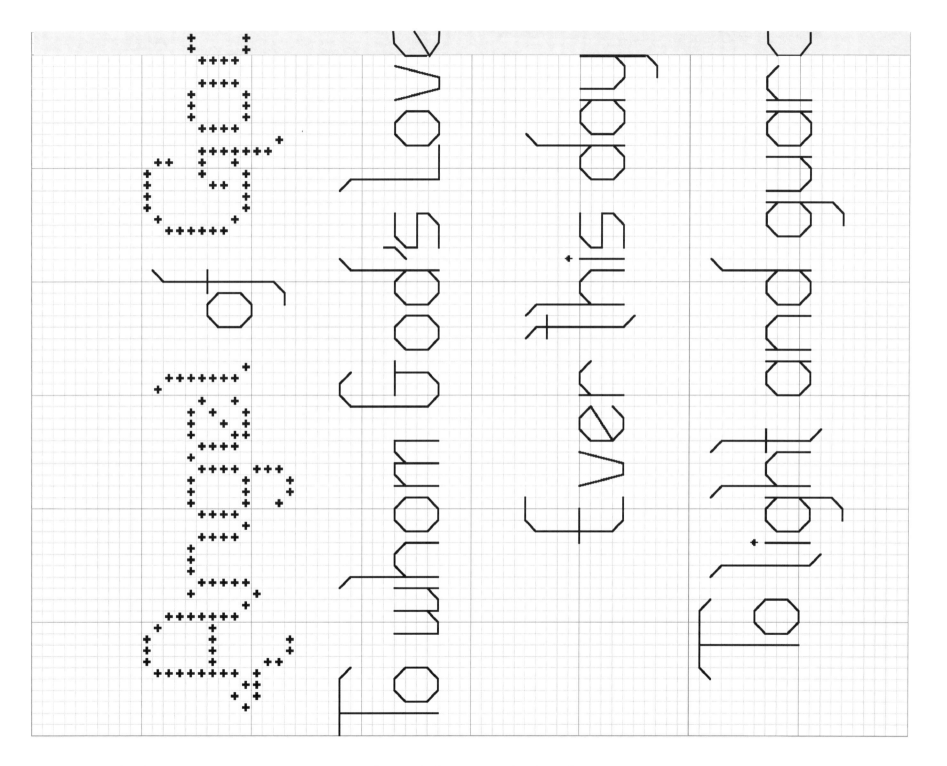

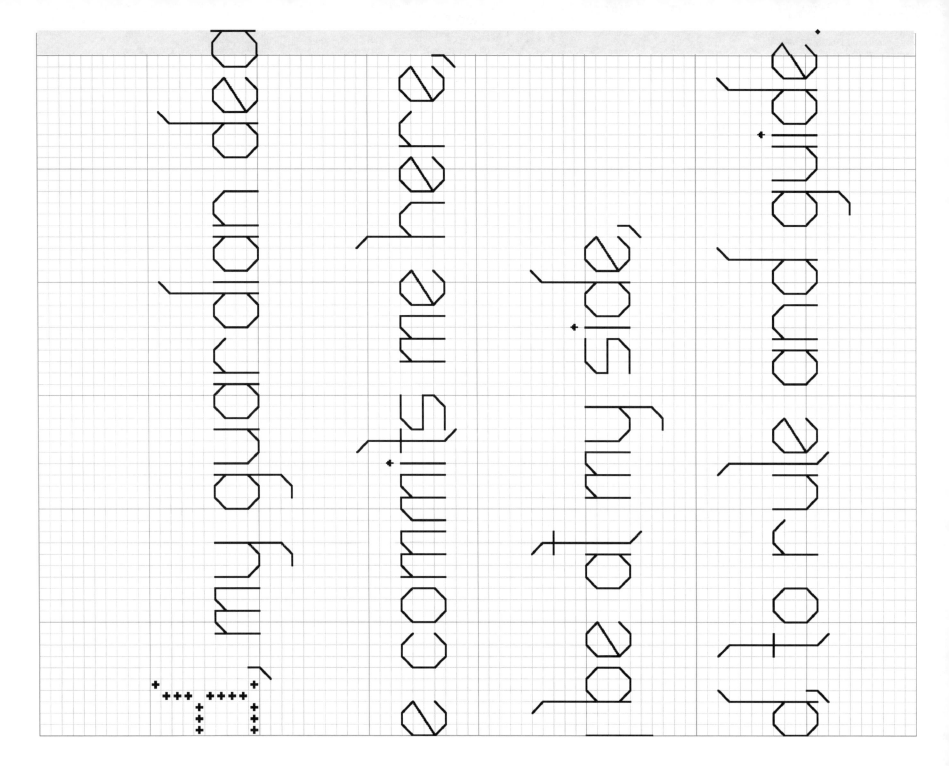

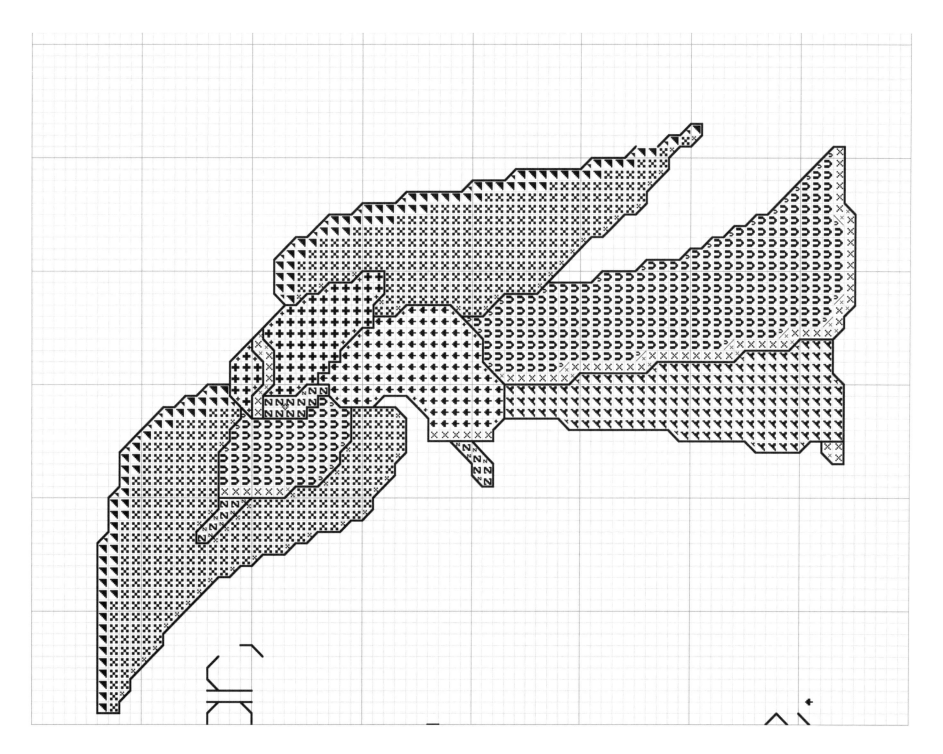

(left margin, rotated) each of us in his own native language? Parthians and Medes and Elamites and residents of Mesopotamia, Judea and

Stained-Glass Pictures

The stained-glass windows in our churches fill their interiors with beautiful colored light, teach the faith by showing images and symbols from the Bible or lives of saints, and may also commemorate benefactors and members of the parish who sponsored their creation. They are beautiful, too.

Stained glass is becoming a popular hobby. There are classes available at many local high schools, community colleges, and art centers that teach this interesting and challenging craft.

An easy and inexpensive alternative to real stained glass are these tissue paper creations that can be hung in windows to make beautiful light (just like the real thing).

This craft's suitability for any age group will depend on the complexity of the image you choose. This craft is probably not suitable for children under four or five (they will find it too frustrating). Children between six and ten will need supervision and, occasionally, help with finicky bits of cutting.

Materials
• Black construction paper, or other sturdy paper
• White or yellow carbon paper, if you can find it
• Colored tissue paper in many colors
  • White glue; and clear tape to mend mistakes
  • Scissors
  • Paintbrush

Directions

Choose a picture you like from the coloring section of this book or from some other source. Lay the white carbon paper on top of the black construction paper and then the picture you have chosen on top of both. Trace over the lines with a ballpoint pen or thick pencil, pressing down hard, to leave white lines below.

If you cannot find carbon paper, press hard enough when tracing over the image to leave indentations marking the lines. Remove the traced image, and draw over the indentations with a light-colored pencil or crayon, something visible on black paper.

Draw a second set of lines about one-fourth inch away from each line on the drawing, to make each part of the drawing into a closed shape.

Starting with a hole punched into the middle of each, cut out the center of each shape, being careful to keep the remaining bars evenly thick throughout the picture.

When you have finished cutting out all the shapes, you should have an outline of your picture that looks like a stained-glass window without the color. (**Optional:** Cut a second sheet of black construction paper in the same manner, so that you have two outline stained-glass sheets.)

Turn the picture over and choose the first space to fill with tissue paper. Cut a piece of tissue paper a bit bigger than the hole. Carefully paint glue around the outline shape and place the tissue paper on the glue, smoothing it as best you can. Let it dry. (It will not take long.) Continue covering the holes with the tissue paper until the entire picture is colored. Use as many or as few colors as you wish.

If you cut a second sheet, carefully paint one side with glue and stick it onto the back of your stained-glass picture to sandwich all the pieces of tissue paper between the two black sheets.

Allow your picture to dry. Hang it in a sunny window.

Happy spring! Happy Easter!

Coloring Pages

"They are filled with new wine." But Peter, standing with the eleven, lifted up his voice and addressed them, "Men of

Lent and Easter in the Domestic Church: Coloring Pages

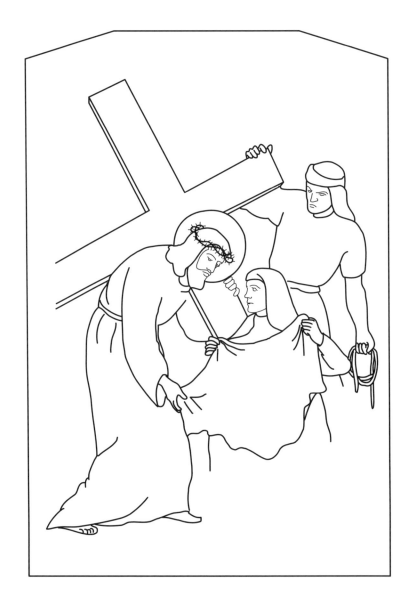

Lent and Easter in the Domestic Church: Coloring Pages

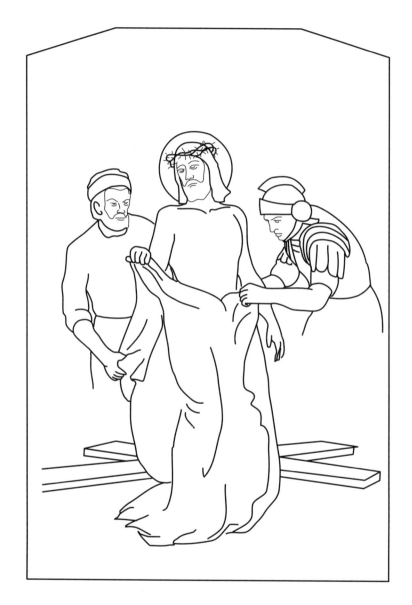

Lent and Easter in the Domestic Church: Coloring Pages

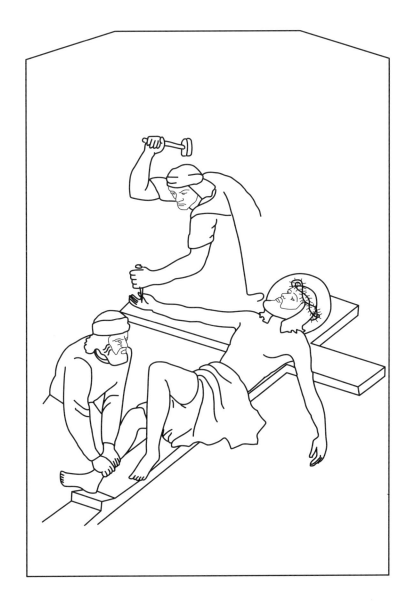

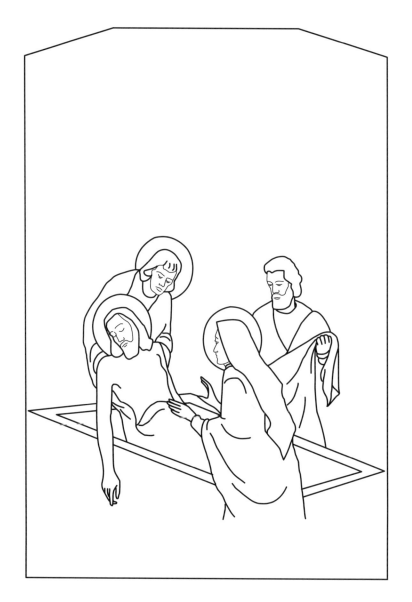

Lent and Easter in the Domestic Church: Coloring Pages

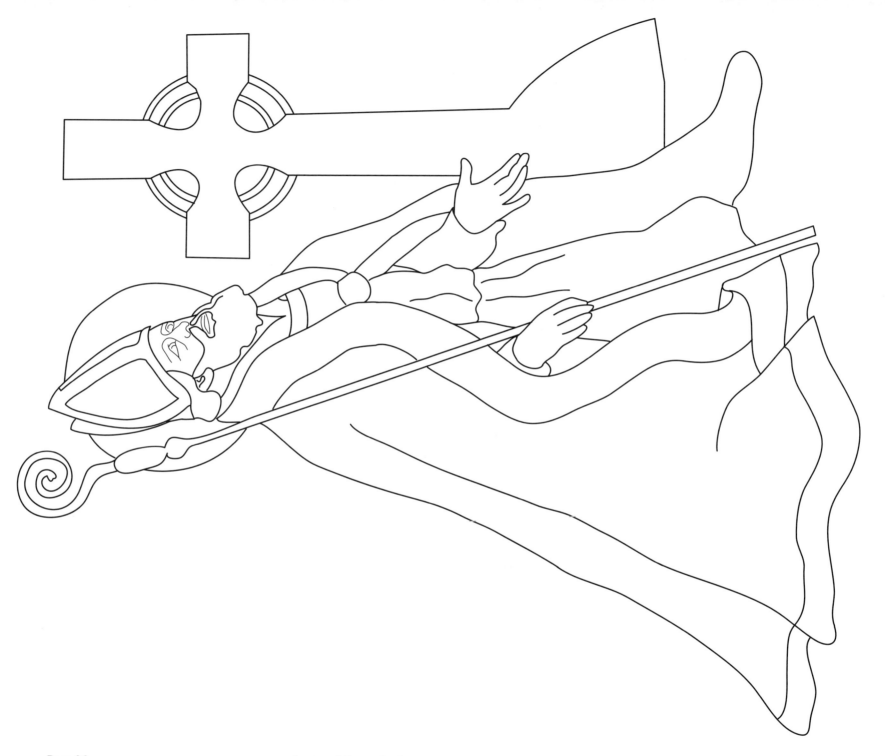

Lent and Easter in the Domestic Church: Coloring Pages

Lent and Easter in the Domestic Church: Coloring Pages

Lent and Easter in the Domestic Church: Coloring Pages

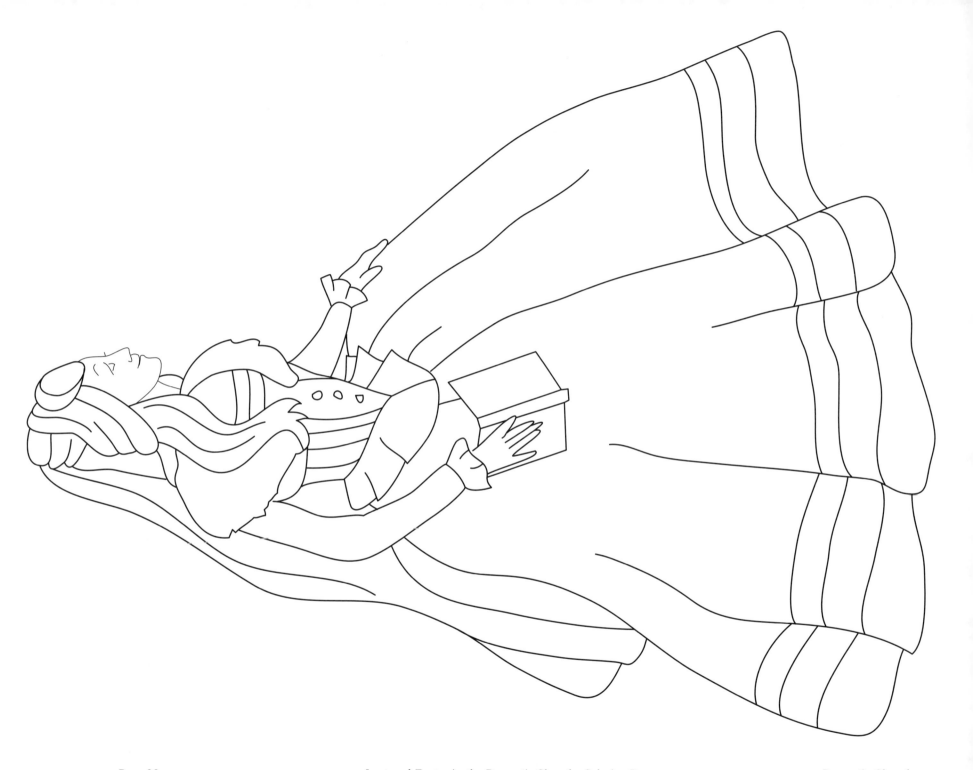

Lent and Easter in the Domestic Church: Coloring Pages

Lent and Easter in the Domestic Church: Coloring Pages

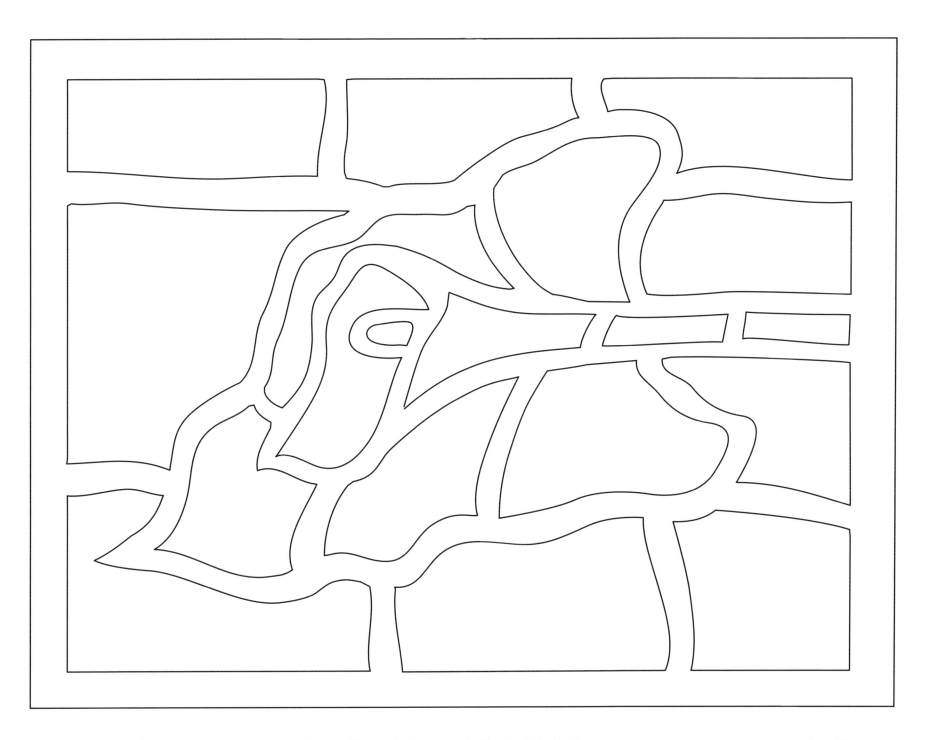

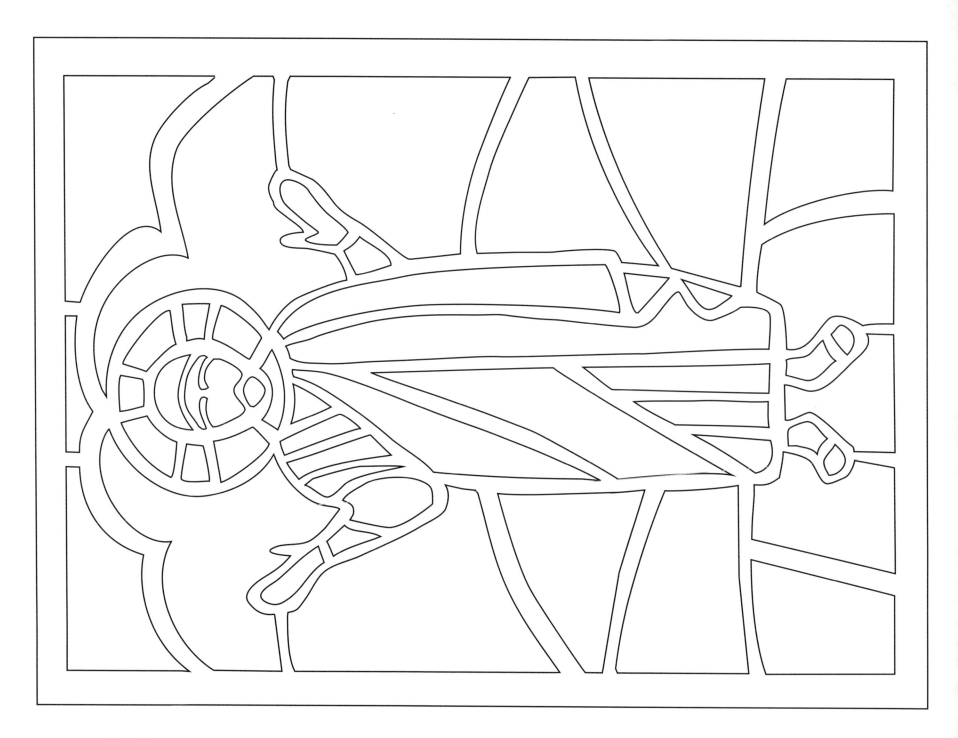

Lent and Easter in the Domestic Church: Coloring Pages

Judea and all who dwell in Jerusalem, let this be known to you, and give ear to my words. For these men are

Additional copies of all coloring pictures and patterns

for your personal use are available at:

http://www.domestic-church.com/index.dir/index_ref_le.htm

Subject Index